Planting Spiritual Seeds

Planting Spiritual Seeds

75 Nature Activities to Help Children and Youth Learn About God

JUDY GATTIS SMITH

Abingdon Press
Nashville

PLANTING SPIRITUAL SEEDS:

NATURE ACTIVITIES TO HELP CHILDREN AND YOUTH LEARN ABOUT GOD

Copyright © 1994 by Abingdon Press

94 95 96 97 98 99 00 01 02 03—10 9 8 7 6 5 4 3 2 1

This book is printed on acid-free recycled paper.

Library of Congress Cataloging-in-Publication Data

Smith, Judy Gattis, 1993–
   Planting spiritual seeds:75 nature activities to help children and youth learn about God / Judy Gattis Smith.
        p. cm.
     Includes index.
     ISBN 0-687-10501-3 (alk. paper)
     1. Nature—Religious aspects—Christianity—Study and teaching. 2. Christian education of children. 3. Children—Religious life.
     I. Title.
BT695.5.S645   1993
268'.432—dc20   93-32019

Scripture quotations, unless otherwise indicated, are from the New Revised Standard Version Bible, copyright © 1989, by the Division of Christian Education of the National Council of the Churches of Christ in the United States of America.
   Those noted KJV are from the King James version of the Bible.

Illustrations by Charles Cox

The poem "Please Touch," by Edwin McMahon and Peter Campbell, is copyright 1969 by Sheed and Ward, Inc.

For Christian Educators I've Known

In my seminars and workshops, I've been blessed to work with many dedicated Christian educators—teachers and pastors with vision, enthusiasm, and tireless zeal. This book is dedicated to them all—with my admiration, my appreciation, and my very best wishes.

Thank you, Jill Reddig, Helen Graves, and Paul Franklyn for putting this book together. Thank you, camp counselors at Camp Alexander Mack, Church of the Brethren, in Milford, Indiana, for trying out these activities—and even finding a devil's fiddle! Thank you, dear family, for your support and encouragement. This book is not *for* you, but *because of* you.

CONTENTS

- -

PREFACE

Our lives are a faint tracing on the surface of mystery.
Annie Dillard, Pilgrim at Tinker's Creek

I was blessed to grow up in a beautiful natural setting in Murfreesboro, Tennessee, in a time when it was safe to wander alone, exploring fields and streams. My homeplace was built over a cave; and in the fields behind the house was Sand Springs, where originally, in the center of deep, clear water, white sand came boiling up through a hole in a rock. By my time, "progress" and attempts to fill in the spring had almost completely destroyed this lovely setting. But for an exploring child, there were still to be found fairy caves and sinkholes and projecting rocks and other things mysterious, wild, and beautiful.

I am blessed again, in my near-retirement years, to find myself in another place of natural beauty—the Blue Ridge Mountains and the Appalachian Trail in Virginia. Here I know the companionship of the Happy Hikers, wise and seasoned adult women who hike weekly in these mountains, opening my eyes to the ever new and astonishing wonders of nature.

I desire that others—especially children—might know the joys of nature discoveries. And so—this book—to deepen a child's love of nature and, by extension, love of God.

INTRODUCTION

- -

There is a weariness about people today, even children. We move sluggishly, as if under a grey cloud. Recreation, pleasure, amusement, and fun do not lift this burden, and they are poor substitutes for joy. Joy, I feel, has its roots in something from which civilization tends to cut us off. It is rooted in God, as experienced through nature and the natural world. There, many of us feel a lifting of the heart and spirit for which mere fresh air and sunshine is not sufficient to account. We feel surging up in us the exuberant, vital feeling of being truly alive.

When Keats spoke of "taking the rainbow out of the sky and clipping the angel's wings," he described our world too well. Yet in children (and in some adults too), there is an instinct for something great and lovely in the world. There are eyes that still see rainbows and angel's wings.

This book is an attempt to get in touch with that instinct, to sensitize, to make us and the children we teach aware that God is present, thinly veiled, in the things of nature: the flower, the rock, the stream. We take our spirituality seriously. God is unknowable, but objects can be known, so we study the objects that God has touched. We look for grass still imprinted with God's footprints, air still fragrant with God's passing.

The ability to see God's activity in everything is our biblical heritage. Where we seem to dwell almost exclusively on secondary causes, the Hebrews seemed to dwell almost exclusively on the Primary cause. In this book, I invite you to join me in affirming that God is the substratum behind everything—the Primary cause.

Nature is a great reservoir of energy, of endless hope and joy. Through the mountains, woods, rivers, trees, plants, and animals, we seek examples that reveal God's greatness and goodness. We approach God through appreciation of all of nature. We affirm that all things owe their existence to God.

How Nature Experiences
Can Help a Child Grow Spiritually

Nature experiences can help by counteracting many of the modern stresses our children face now and will face when they are older.

1. Much of their labor is mental rather than physical. There are days spent thinking actively—solving problems, coping with new information, adapting to change, making decisions. To counteract this, children can be taught to relax and be refreshed through nature. They will learn that not all knowledge can be expressed in words.

2. The world for our children is and will be overloaded with continual learning and change, new and relevant information, erosion of stability. To counteract this, in this book we suggest activities that sensitize children to the permanent, eternal, enduring, and unchanging God. Through nature, we learn that we are a people with roots.

3. The world our children know and will know encourages polyphasic activity (doing two or more things at the same time). They respond to two (and often more) sources of stimulation at once. They are "strung out" by television and advertising "hype" that upset the nervous system. The nature activities in this book help children concentrate on one thing, find a center of deep quiet within themselves, and learn to enjoy simple things. As one man told me, "We go fishing, not catching."

4. To counteract days spent indoors with machines and computers and videos, children are encouraged to be outdoors more, to become aware of things around them, to observe the natural world. We need to look very closely, since the earth teaches us its eternal messages quietly—in a way unlike textbook learning. We ask, "What are you saying to me through nature, Lord? What message are you giving me as I look at nature today?" God's reply may come in a word, a sentence, an image, a burning bush, or a guiding star. We search, hoping that God will see and that our hearts will understand. We seek a treasure that is a mystery.

When and How to Use This Book

This book does not contain curriculum that must be followed from start to finish. I hope you will find material here that will meet a variety of needs and circumstances. For example:

1. SUNDAY SCHOOL

Because most Sunday school classes meet at a specific time in the morning, some activities related to other times of the day may need to be adapted. Instead of watching the sun rise, you may have the class remember seeing the sun rise, or plan to watch the sun rise.

If you are following published curriculum in your classes, you may use these activities to supplement it. Use the Scripture Index to locate activities which relate to specific passages. Or begin each class with a nature activity for six weeks, praising God for all of creation. Or, at the time of year when you can be outdoors, select appropriate activities to make a 30-minute walk also a learning experience.

2. CAMP

A camp setting provides wonderful opportunities to experience God through nature. You may want to choose one activity from each chapter for each day. You will have the advantage of being with children and youth from dawn (chapter one) throughout the day and into the evening (chapter six). There are plenty of inside activities included, so rainy days will not be a problem.

3. VACATION BIBLE SCHOOL

Summer Bible school often provides opportunities for both classroom activities and outdoor activities. Select experiences from the book to fit your timetable. Take advantage of the fact that you will be with the children for several consecutive days and can plan activities that will carry over from one day to the next.

The book is divided into six sections, each of which uses the metaphor of a part of the day to correspond to an aspect of spiritual growth.

Each section contains sensitizing activities that begin with Scripture. This Scripture is the indispensable groundwork and should be read or heard first. Sometimes it is used in a later activity. At other times, it is just to set the tone and focus of the experience. At the end of each chapter, some of the verses used in that section are presented again, affirming that the bare words themselves are powerful and provocative.

Following the Scripture, there is something "To Think About." This reflection, or background information, may be used as a brief personal devotion by the teacher. However, in most cases you will want to share these thoughts with your class, as preparation for the activity that follows, adapting the language to the age level and particular circumstances of your class. In some cases, suggestions for adaptation are provided under "Teaching Helps."

The activities are wide-ranging. Some are to do indoors; some require being outdoors. I have worked to include activities which appeal to all the senses, include images and stories from other cultures, speak to wide age ranges, encourage creative expression and curiosity, and, always, bring children closer to God through nature.

Some activities are followed by "Teaching Helps" or by an idea "To Ponder."

Suggested age levels are not included because I find children and adults to be responsive to a far wider range of experiences than most experts advise. You are encouraged to adapt. Try these experiences intergenerationally.

This is a book not of ecology but of appreciation. Yet, when we can see our everyday surroundings as an endless source of allure, learning, beauty, and even amusement, we are more likely to resist its destruction. If we hurry through the day, seeing nature's backdrop as ordinary and dull, it becomes easier to exploit or destroy these surroundings through pollution or overdevelopment.

As a leader, you are encouraged to make daily discoveries. Curiosity and wonder and eyes that see—these are all we need. This book is for the spiritual development of children through nature, but I hope that it also speaks to the child in each of us.

Chapter One

DAWN

Awakening

■ ■

Let us press on to know the LORD; his appearing is as sure as the dawn.

(HOSEA 6:3)

In this chapter, we are trying to awaken our students and ourselves to life more fully lived—to the possibility of fullness. We are attempting to jump-start their and our awareness of the presence of God in all our lives and in the world, to shake them from the dullness and drowsiness of everyday living. We are saying, "Arise! Get Up! Wake up!"

Wake up, body, to movement! Wake up, ears, to the day's call! Wake up, eyes, to the sight of a new day! Wake up, spirit, to an awareness of who you are—you are a child of God!

Open your eyes and your hearts! Open up to life within us and around us. An untried day awaits us. Awake! Arise! Go forth with anticipation, excitement, exuberance, with joy and hope. We cannot hazard a guess as to what will happen next. What will the weather be? Which wild flower will bloom in unexpected places?

This is the day that the Lord has made.
(The time we have is NOW.)
Let us rejoice and be glad in it.
(The place we have is HERE.)

Following are some exercises in awakening. Alertness and awareness are critical to spirituality. Whatever time of day you do these activities, the feeling is DAWN.

1. When You Run to Greet the Dawn

Focusing Scripture

Get you up to a high mountain,
   O Zion, herald of good tidings;
lift up your voice with strength,
   O Jerusalem, herald of good tidings . . .
say to the cities of Judah,
   "Here is your God!"

(ISAIAH 40:9)

Peter got up and ran to the tomb.

(LUKE 24:12)

Then the Spirit said to Philip, "Go over to this chariot and join it." So Philip ran up to it.

(ACTS 8:29-30a)

To Think About

We have an immediate, running response to dawn. We go eagerly. We rush to do the bidding of the Spirit.

Think about the things you run to greet—a person? An event you look forward to? Running is an appropriate way to greet the dawn, the new day.

The exuberant joy of a new day is expressed in this Papago Native American chant:

> A low range of mountains,
> Toward them I'm running.
> From the top of these mountains
> I shall see the dawn.

Activity

The class members join hands in a large circle. Running in place, they repeat this sentence three times, in unison:

> A low range of mountains,
> Toward them I'm running.

Now, with a running step, they circle left, again repeating the sentence three times. Then they circle right, once more chanting the sentence three times.

The people drop hands and run to the center of the circle. Each person raises both hands overhead, palms facing up, face looking up. The teacher says:

> From the top of the mountain,
> I shall see the Dawn.

Standing on tiptoe, stretching as high as possible, the class repeats that sentence three times, then returns to the original circle.

Teacher: Now, with gestures, we will experience Ecclesiastes 3:11. God has made everything beautiful. The class imitates the teacher:

> God (arms outstretched to heaven)
> made (tap right fist on left fist)
> beautiful (circle face with right index finger while smiling).

Teacher: Welcome to a new day. Here we are, world. Here we are, Lord. The day awaits us!

Teaching Help

If children with handicaps are unable to circle, have them clap the rhythm and join in the chanting.

If adults are doing this activity, instruct them to remember the childhood freedom of running and try to capture that feeling.

AND GOD SAID, "IT IS GOOD."

2. When You Name Wake Robin

Focusing Scripture

> *The Lord God planted a garden in Eden, in the east.*
> (GENESIS 2:8)

To Think About

An early spring wild flower in many parts of the country is the trillium. The leaves and flower parts grow in threes, and for this reason some call it the trinity flower. More than thirty species can be found in northern woods and bogs and on southern mountains. A deep red trillium found in late April and early May near where I live is called Wake Robin. What could better describe the spirit of dawn and spring?

Activity

With your class, create names for other flowers.
Step 1: If possible, go on a spring hike to discover wild flowers. If this is not possible, look at pictures of wild flowers found in flower identification books, covering up the names. Show pictures of Wake Robin.
Step 2: The class studies the flower or picture, thinking of "dawn" and "spring" words—words that capture the spirit of awakening.
Step 3: Name the flower. First choose a verb, such as "wake." Then choose a noun, such as "Robin." The color and the size may help in naming the flower, but be sure the name captures "dawn" or "spring" associations.
Step 4: Share the names. In your own words, say to the group: Naming is a way of capturing an essence. To name is to try for understanding. Seeing a trillium is a lovely experience. You can "name" that experience. A careful observer of nature is a "Namer." Amid the bogglement of similar but not identical things, we recognize by naming. We feel our way into the budding of spring. When we name things, we have a more thoughtful relationship with them.
Step 5: Choose ten wild flowers that grow in your area and learn their names.

To Wonder About

Do things know their names? In an apocryphal expansion of the Genesis story, not only did Adam name the animals, but the moment he did, each recognized its name and came when called.

Use your imagination. Think of each flower as recognizing its name, shaking its head if the name is wrong, nodding agreeably if the name is correct.

AND GOD SAID, "IT IS GOOD."

3. When You Consider New Life—Yours and the Day

Focusing Scripture

> *I praise you, for I am fearfully and wonderfully made.*
> (PSALM 139:14a)

To Think About

Each new rising of the sun is tantamount to a new life, a time new and different from that which had passed the previous day.

We don't know what each day will bring. As I am writing this book, I am waiting for a grandchild to be born. If you have had such an experience, recall your feelings. Each day on waking, I think, "Will this be the day? Will that new life emerge today?"

And I realize that every day can begin like this—with great anticipation and expectation. New life for us in many forms may begin today—and does. Each morning represents a new start in life. Out of darkness rises a new time.

The birth of a child is analogous to the coming of dawn. The same joy and hope is present. Like a new day, the child has a life to live and purpose to fulfill. There is a promise and a freshness, and a new beginning with each birth.

Activity

The teacher says: Each of us was born with these gifts: life and purpose. Class members fill out the following:

Think about your birth.

Place _____

Date _____

What story were you told about your birth? _____

Do you recall the birth of a brother or sister? _____

Do you have a baby brother or sister now? _____

How are you alike? _____

How are you different? _____

Teaching Help

This is especially effective if a member of the class is celebrating a birthday. For younger children, discuss the questions above orally. For older children, you also may want to ask:

____Why do you think you were born, fresh and unique, into the world?

____Do you have an inkling of what your purpose in life might be?

____How does one person reach God's potential, while another does not?

The teacher directs a silent meditation with these words:

All young things have inside them the plan for the shape they will become. So do you. Did you know that one thing that separates things that are alive from things that are not, is that alive things grow from the inside out? What God plans for you to be is growing inside you now. Can you feel it happening? Is something in you awakening?

Watch for things in nature growing in their own time and way. Growth (spiritual and physical) can't be programmed or hurried. Think what would happen to a chick if we tried to hurry its birth by picking the shell off the egg. We trust God, and in God's time, we will grow and become what God plans for us to be.

Think about this: No stage of life can be rushed or skipped, so live fully in the stage where you are now.

With the beginning of each day, think: I too am unique and new to the world.

> You clothed me with skin and flesh,
>   and knit me together with bones and sinews.
> You have granted me life and steadfast love,
>   and your care has preserved my spirit.
>
> *(JOB 10:11, 12)*

AND GOD SAID, "IT IS GOOD."

4. When You Welcome the Day

Focusing Scripture

> *Every day I will bless you,*
>   *and praise your name forever and ever.*
>
> (PSALM 145:2)

To Think About

You can individually greet the dawn each morning. Get up before sunrise to prepare. Stand facing the east and watch dawn approaching. Raise your arms the moment the sun breaks above the horizon, and repeat Isaiah 60:1, shouting it to the new day, if possible:

> (I will) "Arise, shine; for your light has come,
>   and the glory of the LORD has risen upon." (me).

Then kiss your fingertips and fling your fingers to the sky. Turn and repeat, facing north and south and west.

Address creation directly. Praise God for the sun and moon, for all the shining stars, for the highest heavens, mountains, and hills, for all wild beasts and all tame animals.

Say thank you to the new day, for the power of warmth and light both from the sun and from God. There is joy in feeling warmth come into the world. Feel rising within you this exuberance for a new day. Awake to a loving and attentive Mystery. The new day is here. You do not need to work for it. You need only receive it and enjoy it. We do not need to find God—only be aware that God is with us.

Remember that the light and warmth are for all people, for all living things, and for yourself. Have you ever seen selective sunshine picking out the righteous? Have you ever seen drops of rain like guided missles, looking for their target of righteous people?

God causes the sun to shine on the just and the unjust. Know that it is a good day.

If you have access to a swing, get in it and swing as high as you can. Think of the sun climbing to the top of the sky.

A moving story came to light after the release of the Iranian hostages. One person explained that they survived captivity by saying to themselves each morning: "Today I choose joy."

If that was possible under such trying circumstances, should we not rejoice with the beginning of each day? We are called to be joyful. We can choose joy.

Activity

Say in your own words: There is a basic rhythm in the body that we, in our modern daily living, do not experience. It is a rhythm that is in harmony with natural settings. We are jolted by the morning rhythms of blaring radios, bonging clocks, and whirring appliances. It is a problem of noise pollution. Excessive noise dulls all our senses and jars us out of the rhythm that should be within us. These noises are at odds with a rhythm that is deeper.

Find your pulse beat. Listen carefully to it to get your special unique rhythm. After finding your pulse, stand silently with your eyes closed, experiencing the pulsations. Then move your feet sideways, one at a time, with each beat of your pulse. Think of your pulse beat as the heartbeat of the earth. Think of yourself as getting in rhythm with the whole earth. You might want to say a word of praise with each pulse beat and foot stomp, such as "joy—joy—joy" or "awake—awake—awake." Think that everything you do today can be natural and in tune with life.

AND GOD SAID, "IT IS GOOD."

5. When Birds Call Your Name

Focusing Scripture

> *Look at the birds of the air . . . your heavenly Father feeds them.*
> (MATTHEW 6:26)

To Think About

Early in the morning, listen as the birds usher in the dawn. At sunrise there is a cacophony of singing called the Dawn Chorus. What better captures the elation of a new day—a new beginning with praise!

Listen for your name in a bird song. The songs of birds—the cadence, speed, and repeated rhythm sometimes sound like the calling of a name. There is the "Peter, Peter, Peter" call of the black-capped chickadee and the "Pretty, Pretty, Pretty (Betty?)" chirp of the cardinal. "Drink your tea," the Towhee seems to say, and the rooster's "Cock-a-doodle-do" tells the world a new day is here.

Augustine was converted when he heard unseen children seeming to sing, "Take up and read." He then picked up his Bible, opened it, and felt that he received a direct message from God.

Perhaps the bird chorus has a direct message for you. What is your song for the day? Listen with the ears of your heart. The trusting joy of morning bird song reminds us of a simple truth that is a profound metaphysical reality: We all belong to God. In God, we live, move, have our being, and live this day.

Pray that just as the birds awaken us to a new day, you will awake to life in a deeper way. Awaken with the singing of birds and the singing within you to a direct word from God.

We listen to a song and are called to a response. Add your song. Perhaps your class would like to sing "Morning Has Broken."

Activity

Here are some ideas you can use to help the birds. In early spring, the class can bring in bits of ribbon, string, yarn, dryer lint, even clippings from their hair. Use mesh bags such as oranges come in to contain the material, and hang the bags in trees near your classroom, if possible. Perhaps you will be lucky enough to see birds help themselves to your building supplies.

In late fall, collect abandoned nests. Since most bird nests are used for one season only, there is no harm in taking an obviously deserted one. Place the nest in a sealed box with mothballs for two weeks, to rid it of pests. Then display the nest on a wonder table. Does it contain bits and pieces from your nest-building bag?

Ask the children not to throw away those crumbs that remain in the bottom of their cereal boxes. Bring them to scatter for the birds to eat.

Sometimes children discover bird feathers outdoors. These can be displayed in an interesting way on a strip of corrugated cardboard taped to the wall. The regular series of lines show off each feather to advantage.

It is interesting that even in large cities you can hear morning bird songs. Sometimes you must listen carefully above early morning noises, but they are still there—the birds are singing.

AND GOD SAID, "IT IS GOOD."

6. When Morning Dew Becomes Holy Water

Focusing Scripture

> *O dwellers in the dust, awake and sing for joy!*
> *For your dew is a radiant dew.*
>
> (ISAIAH 26:19*b, c*)

To Think About

A unique dawn phenomenon and joy is dew. There it is on bright mornings, turning the grass to sparkling diamonds. It evokes an infectious sense of wonder. Dew forms on the grass when the air above is cool and dry, and the air near the ground is warm and damp.

Go out barefoot into the dew-covered grass. Feel the moisture and freshness. Look for morning spiderwebs that are pure beauty when jeweled with morning dewdrops.

Teaching Help

The following activity works best at camp or when you are with children overnight.

Activity

Dig a shallow hole. Before dark, line the sides of your hole with a plastic garbage bag. Anchor the bag around the hole with rocks to hold it in place. The next morning, lift the bag out carefully and pour the dew that has collected into a paper cup.

Read I Chronicles 11:15-19 to the class or tell it in your own words:

Three of the thirty chiefs went down to the rock to David at the cave of Adulam, while the army of Philistines was encamped in the valley of Rephaim. David was then in the stronghold; and the garrison of the Philistines was then at Bethlehem. David said longingly, "O that someone would give me water to drink from the well of Bethlehem that is by the gate!" Then the Three broke through the camp of the Philistines, and drew water from the well of Bethlehem that was by the gate, and they brought it to David. But David would not drink of it; he poured it out to the LORD, and said, "My God forbid that I should do this. Can I drink the blood of these men? For at the risk of their lives they brought it." Therefore he would not drink it. The three warriors did these things.

Ask: "Have you ever received such a precious gift? What is the most precious gift you have ever received? Would you give the most precious gift you have ever received to God?"

Think about how special that cup of water was to David. God gives us the same unmeasurable precious gift of dew each morning.

Just as David poured his water on the ground as libation to God, so we pour out our cup of dew in appreciation beyond words for all God has done for us.

AND GOD SAID, "IT IS GOOD."

7. When You Get Up on the Wrong Side of the Bed

Focusing Scripture

> *It is now the moment for you to wake from sleep. . . . The night is far gone, the day is near.*
> (ROMANS 13:11a, 12a)

To Think About

On some days, we wake up depressed. We feel fatigued and somber. Perhaps a fleeting dream saddened us. A gray mood seems to envelop us.

Let yourself become aware of the way a day begins in nature. At dawn, the flowers open, the birds begin to twitter, a spectacular show of color and light approaches with the sun. Activity replaces the quiet of the night. Nature seems to begin each day with great creative energy and praise to God.

Learn from nature. Begin the day slowly. Practice making your first thought of the day praise and thanks to God for the watchful care of the night and the gift of a new day. What is the very first thing you say—the first words you utter? Practice saying first of all: "Thank you for the gift of life and for another day."

This is another morning of creation. The world has been visibly recreated during the night.

Activity

Invite the class members to sit quietly with their eyes closed. Say:

Let your imagination carry you to mornings that are beginning around the world. In the ocean, sea gulls are dipping and calling. Whales and dolphins are leaping for joy. On mountaintops, wild goats are jumping gleefully. In the savannahs of Africa, gazelles prance. In the rain forest, colorful parrots dart among orchids that grow before your eyes. Twirlybirds hop straight up in the air.

The trees around the world are clapping their hands, and mountains are singing with joy. All around the world, in deserts and on ice floes and tropical islands, morning is coming. Think of Psalm 148:9-10, 13*a*:

> Mountains and all hills,
>   fruit trees and all cedars!
> Wild animals and all cattle,
>   creeping things and flying birds! . . .
> Let them praise the name of the LORD.

You too are a part of this waking nature. Now call to mind its beauties. From your imagination, draw up the beautiful images stored there: snow on a high mountain, reflections in a placid lake, a field of laughing flowers. Remember that you too are a part of the beauties of nature. Affirm the beauty in yourself: "I am . . . wonderfully made" (Ps. 139:14*a*).

Slowly stretch your arms and legs. Hear God saying, "You are beautiful, made in my image, an expression of my love. Do not condemn yourself or judge yourself so harshly. My love revealed in you is beauty." Pray as someone once suggested: "O God, help me believe the truth about myself, no matter how beautiful it is."

The sense of sadness may still be with you. It may not be a day when you can shout and sing and run, but you can be in touch with a deep confidence of God's love. To be alive and part of this wonderful, changing universe is a reason to arise.

AND GOD SAID, "IT IS GOOD."

8. When Spring Comes Suddenly

Focusing Scripture

> *When you send forth your spirit, they are created;*
> *and you renew the face of the ground.*
>
> (PSALM 104:30)

To Think About

Winter always seems long, and then when Spring comes, the changes in nature happen suddenly. It is fun to watch for these sudden appearances and to track and note and mark these changes. We can all be spring detectives.

- Who can see the first robin? And where? Are your ears sharp enough to catch the difference in a robin's song in spring? The reassuring voice that sounds so sweet and clear seems to be saying, "Fear not, fear not"—a wonderful affirmation that winter is past.
- Who can find the first ladybug of the season?
- Can you catch the day when the willow tree suddenly shows that tender yellow-green of early spring?
- Do you suddenly notice that the bare limbs of trees have a deep maroon hue?
- What night do you hear the first spring peepers, with their astonishingly loud cry?
- Who can find the first pale wild flower? Small violets are among the first flowers. Spring beauties are tiny wild flowers that seem to open hesitantly. On sunny days they smile openly. On cloudy or cool days, they close up tight. Snowdrops in white and green lie close to the ground.
- Who can find the first cultivated flower? Tiny crocus in purple and gold sometimes peep up through snow.
- Who can spot the first fuzzy fiddleheads of young ferns, pushing up through dead leaves in the woods? A child I know calls them "rolled-up party snappers."
- Who notices the sap when it begins to run in the trees?
- Who notices the return of the bees?
- Who is first to hear the sound of ice breaking and of water beginning to swirl around rocks and tree stumps in clogged creeks?
- Who can find the first pussy willow?
- Can you feel spring in the air?

March 21 is the first day of spring. What is it like in your area, and who can see it first? Be a spring detective. What clues of spring can you find?

Celebrate the sudden return of any or all of the above things. Their full significance hits us when we have seen the same place when it was bare and winterbound. Now the transformation has occurred overnight. Things are happening around us that shift just enough to suggest a new pattern—a new chance—a new beginning. It is this mystery of growth and life that excites us and gives us hope. It is this beauty and sweetness and color and freshness starting forth so suddenly and bravely that has power over us. There seems to be no dullness anywhere visible or thinkable.

This can speak to us of God. Let this freshness become part of your life. Let newness break through. Open yourself to a momentary response to wonder, as you look at the sudden changes in nature. Remember that our God can suddenly change our cold, brittle lives, too. There is always hope and a new beginning.

Activity

Choose any or all of the "firsts" listed above, or others appropriate for your area, and ask your class to discover them. You might make a chart to record the new things of spring. Then celebrate them. Yellow seems to be spring's favorite color, so light yellow candles, cover the worship table with a yellow cloth, force some forsythia. Wear yellow clothes. Eat lemon cupcakes.

Frame a "Spring's Beginning" picture. Give a piece of cardboard to each student and instruct them to cut a square or rectangular hole in the center. Take the class outdoors and go looking for one of the spring's beginning objects mentioned above. Use the cardboard frames as viewfinders to focus in on the object.

Say: We try to capture the moment, but the powerful message that comes to us is that nature refuses to stay the same. It suddenly bursts forth in new form—and so must we.

AND GOD SAID, "IT IS GOOD."

9. When Clouds Announce Weather

Focusing Scripture

The Pharisees and Sadducees came, and to test Jesus they asked him to show them a sign from heaven. He answered them, "When it is evening, you say, 'It will be fair weather, for the sky is red.' And in the morning, 'It will be stormy today, for the sky is red and threatening.' You know how to interpret the appearance of the sky, but you cannot interpret the signs of the times."

(MATTHEW 16:1-3)

To Think About

At the beginning of a day, we usually check the weather. What will it be like today? What shall I wear?

Some people look at the clouds to help them forecast the weather. Good weather clouds are high clouds or woolly puffs. Clouds that look like wisps of hair or feathers are considered fair-weather clouds. Storm clouds are dark and tall, with flat tops. Layered clouds that lie low often bring precipitation. Some people think that clouds indicate a changing weather pattern. Folk chants express these ideas:

> Mackerel sky, mackerel sky
> Not long wet, not long dry.
> OR
> A sunny shower
> Won't last half an hour.

Activity

1. Draw a cloud picture of your spirit to illustrate your agenda for the day.

Draw woolly puffs. Write on them what you could do for God today. Draw storm clouds. Shade them gray. Label them with the problems or difficulties you may face today. Draw feathery clouds. Write on them your personal agenda for the day. Study your picture. Does your personal agenda get in the way of God's agenda? How do they affect the trouble areas?

You can make your picture more elaborate by using cotton balls for the clouds: Bunch up for puffy clouds; stretch out for wispy clouds. Use white glue to hold them in place. Add a little gray paint to storm clouds.

Now behind the clouds that shadow us daily, draw the brilliance of a rainbow, indicating the promises and power and faithfulness of God. As John Wesley once said, "The best of all—God is with us."

2. Bill Zimmermann's book *Make Beliefs* contains an exercise that challenges you to make believe you could invent a new season. And he asks: What kind of weather would there be?

Carrying this a step further, can you imagine a new kind of cloud in the sky? What would be its shape? Its color?

Our Sunday school class could think of no new colors. We had seen all the shades of red, purple, orange, pink, and its many variations, in the sunrise and sunset. We had seen the black, brown, and gray tones in storm clouds. We decided that blue clouds would be lost in the blues of the sky, and green would just look like extensions of trees and green horizons. One student had read that there are many more colors in the universe than our eyes are able to see. We cannot do much more than begin to grasp the beauty of our God.

3. Keep a weather chart with your class. List all the good things about every kind of day, to help the children focus positively on the weather. For example, rain helps crops, and so on.

AND GOD SAID, "IT IS GOOD."

DAWN
Awakening

I praise you, for I am fearfully and wonderfully made.

(PSALM 139:14*a*)

It is now the moment for you to wake from sleep. . . . The night is far gone, the day is near.

(ROMANS 13:11*a*, 12*a*)

Look at the birds of the air . . . your heavenly Father feeds them.

(MATTHEW 6:26)

Every day I will bless you,
   and praise your name forever and ever.

(PSALM 145:2)

The LORD God planted a garden in Eden, in the east.

(GENESIS 2:8)

Let us press on to know the LORD;
   his appearing is as sure as the dawn.

(HOSEA 6:3)

Chapter Two

MORNING

Discovering Beauty

▬ ▬

Having awakened spiritually, we go forth to discover—to respond to the day ahead, and to God in that day. We look long and deep at what we find. What will be unveiled and revealed? Discovery arises from conviction—that there is something there to be found.

In our adventures we do not particularly seek information. We do not want to be too precise or scientific about birds and trees and flowers and water. We go with an openness to the sheer enjoyment of these things, asking: What speaks to us of God?

> To open yourself to meadow and morning
> to what is before you
> is to find Emmanuel
> to know God—with us
> as life in the moment.
> *Edwin McMahon and Peter Campbell,*
> *"Please Touch"*

Recently I went on a hike to a beautiful waterfall. The wild flowers growing near were unusually large and abundant. Dutchman's-pipes, with their pipe-shaped flowers and beautifully twined stems, climbed luxuriously up trees. Jack-in-the-pulpits almost three feet high were growing straight out of a rock outcropping. Bleeding hearts splashed red in the sunlight.

Suddenly the air was rent with shouts as a whole class of third-graders ran by, straight up the steep, rocky path.

"Wait!" I called. "Did you see the jacks? Did you see the pipes? Did you see the hearts?"

"No, No," they shouted. "We're going to the top."

"Well," I thought, "at least they will have a spectacular view."

No sooner had the last child passed than I heard the running steps of the first children returning.

"Did you see the view?" I called.

"No, no," they panted in passing. "We have to hurry and get back to school to catch the bus."

I stood amazed as the stampede rushed back down the mountain. I'm sure that running in the fresh, crisp air and jumping over slippery rocks was fun, but I sighed at what they had missed—wonders that were right before them.

This experience convinced me that children (and perhaps all of us) must be directed and helped to see—to discover, to uncover, to spy, to open our eyes to the awesomeness around us. And that is the purpose of this section.

The activities here are best experienced in or near a wooded area. Outdoors, we can become a part of the natural world. Usually we need go no farther than a nearby woods. These activities use wild flowers, plants, and nature objects. If it is impossible to include an outdoor excursion, be creative! Use pictures or slides of the wild flowers, plants, and mushrooms. Bring in examples of twig critters and natural imperfections. The activities and discussions can take place in your classroom. The feeling is Morning and Discovery.

1. Aaron's Rod

Focusing Scripture

> *Teach me your way, O LORD,*
> *that I may walk in your truth.*
>
> (PSALM 86:11)

To Think About

Before venturing into the woods, spend some time talking about the natural environment you will be visiting. Outdoor activities often erupt into a joyous explosion of energy, and children scatter into the far reaches of an outdoor area. For this reason, be sure to define clearly the boundaries beyond which they may not explore. Explain how you will travel together through the wooded area.

This is a good time to remind your class that we never litter. "Pack it in—Pack it out" is the rule. Explain that walking quietly and avoiding loud noises may bring unexpected surprises. In the following activities, though you are looking for a particular assignment, give other "looking for" assignments as the class hikes along together—for example, heart-shaped leaves or flowers. Be open to the unplanned happenings and spur-of-the-moment inspirations. Often these turn out to be the best part.

Good, sturdy shoes make walking in the woods more enjoyable, as does rubbing in a good bug repellant.

As teachers and leaders, we can set the mood for these activities by speaking in gentle and intense voices. We wish to convey wonder and stimulate awe, to cultivate alertness to the spiritual meanings of what we discover.

Activity

Explain to your students that they are going forth to make discoveries in God's world that will help them make discoveries in their spiritual world. Be flexible, and have a good time.

PREPARING FOR THE JOURNEY

1. Each person will need a walking stick. Read the story of Aaron's flowering staff in Numbers 17:1-11.

2. The students can prepare their own walking sticks or staffs, using driftwood from the river or dead branches from the yard, or even broom handles. These can be cut to a walking-stick length for each particular student.

Instruct the students to write their names on their walking sticks, using felt-tipped markers. Then, remembering the Bible story, they may decorate their staffs any way they choose—with flowers, buds, blossoms, fruit, or with a vine winding up the stick.

Compare our physical journey with our spiritual journey. As the students are working, ask them to think about the great amount of time, effort, and patience it takes for a plant to grow, to bud, to blossom, then bear fruit. Suggest that we need to spend just as much time on our spiritual life, if we want to grow.

When the decorating is finished, place all the staffs together in the center of a circle. Then dedicate the staffs:

Leader: We dedicate these staffs as reminders that we walk with the Lord. As the staffs of the early Israelites reminded them to end their complaints against God, we pray that we also may trust and have faith that God is with us in all places and at all times.
All: "Let your good spirit lead me on a level path" (Ps. 143:10*b*).

Activity

You can make and take with you some Aaron Rod cookies, if you desire a snack on your hike. Prepare or buy a long roll of sugar-cookie dough. Using the candy flowers found in packages of birthday-cake decoration kits, let the class decorate the roll, pressing the "flowers" into the "rods." Then slice the dough and bake according to instructions. While the cookies are baking, talk to the class about how to walk in the woods. When the cookies are done, take them with you into the woods.

AND GOD SAID, "IT IS GOOD."

SPECIAL PREPARATION FOR WILDFLOWER EXPERIENCES

Before the next three wildflower experiences, read this section. Jesus said, "Consider the lilies of the field." In the first series of discoveries, we use wild flowers to speak to us of God.

Wildflowers grow almost everywhere—in fields, meadows, along the roads, in and around ponds and streams and rivers, in the woods—even between cracks in city sidewalks. They are wonderful and extravagant gifts which nature showers upon us.

Ideally, these discoveries should take place out of doors. A classroom is second best to the whole experience of being outside in a natural setting—the panorama of the sky above, punctuated with clouds, the temperature and atmosphere felt through our pores, the fragrance of nature all around us. The earliest spring days are particularly pleasant. We walk out to adventure. We see a flower, as if for the first time.

We slow down and wonder that we are a part of all this. We use the familiar (trees, flowers, plants) to talk about the unfamiliar (God). We tune ourselves to the daily and hourly miracle of usually unnoticed beauty that is close at hand. You can help to cultivate a sensitivity in your students that will grow into an enduring respect. These outdoor times are often followed by a sharpening of appreciation.

Ralph Waldo Emerson said, "The eye reads omens where it goes." The wildflowers suggested as omens in the following activities may not grow in your area, although I tried to choose those found commonly over a wide area. Feel free to substitute your local flowers in these activities. If an outdoor experience is impossible, pictures of the suggested wildflowers may be used.

Wildflowers make interesting scrapbooks, particularly for older children. They will enjoy drawing and identifying flowers, cataloging their leaf shape and particular characteristics. There are even series of American wildflowers on stamps. Your class may wish to collect and study these. For our purposes (using wildflowers to make us more spiritually aware), always add this to each page of the scrapbook: How does this flower point us to God? What message from God might we read in this flower?

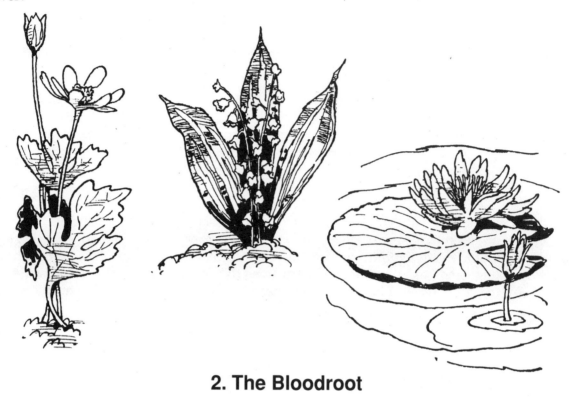

2. The Bloodroot

Focusing Scripture

The earth will disclose the blood shed on it.

(ISAIAH 26:21*c*)

To Think About

Many of our Bible stories, particularly in the Old Testament, are full of wars and killings, and it puzzles us to read these stories. When Jesus was born, King Herod was so angry and jealous that he killed all the baby boys around Bethlehem who were under two years of age, hoping to kill Jesus, and apparently not even caring how many others. Perhaps there is something in all of us, hidden like roots, that is barbaric and cruel. We know that violence and terror are a very real part of many lives.

Talk with your class about violence and terror in their own neighborhoods. What do they fear? What about violence on television or in movies? How do they feel about that? Have they experienced violence at school? Let the class members share experiences and fears. Think with the class about the crucifixion of Jesus and the part malicious stupidity played in his death.

Hold up a picture of the bloodroot and talk about the delicate, white, scented flower.

Say: We will use this flower to remind us of a message from God. It reminds us that we can rise above ugly, bloody things. We are called to something far lovelier. The bloodroot says, "No more killings, Lord. Not again. Purify us all." We are meant to be blossoms, not roots.

Read the Bible verse. Look closely and ponder the bloodroot. Ask God to give you the gift of understanding. If the mystery deepens, it is because we view it more closely and with clearer vision.

Activity

If bloodroot grows in your area (all along the east coast, west to Texas, and north to North Dakota) take a woods walk, searching for this early spring flower. From two to eight inches above ground, its snow-white petals glisten in the sunlight. The petals are delicate, with a golden center. Ask someone with knowledge of the flower and the location to lead you. It is often hidden deep in the woods. It opens in the sun and closes at night. You will have to push away the dead, damp, clinging leaves to see the root. The stout underground stem bleeds red when cut open, the "blood" referred to in the name. After the leader has pointed out the flower, allow the children to search for others. They often grow in clusters.

Activity

Make a peace window. Ask permission to pick a bloodroot. If there are clusters in the woods, it will not hurt to pick one or two. Caution: The plant is a skin irritant to some, and the "blood" in the stem may stain. When cutting, step carefully so that you do not destroy other plants around the one you want. With scissors, gently cut the blossom and stem only. Leave the root. The flower perishes quickly, so put it in a plastic bag until you get back to your classroom. Try to keep the bag out of direct sunlight and begin working on it immediately.

Work on an ironing board covered with a towel. Place the flower on a piece of waxed paper. Cover with a second sheet of waxed paper. Set the iron on the lowest setting and iron the waxed paper close to the flower, but not touching it. This seals the flower in place. Cover the whole thing with brown paper (such as from a paper sack) and press all over.

Hang the flower in your church school window so that the light shines through it. Let the picture speak to you of God and the victory of love over hate, peace over violence.

While bloodroot is a more unusual wild flower, many "weeds" that are lovely wildflowers grow in abundance: Queen Anne's lace, ox-eye daisies, dandelions. These are good flowers to use in projects in which the whole class participates. If you wish, these flowers can be picked on your hike and, following the above procedure, all the students can create window hangings to surround the peace window.

AND GOD SAID, "IT IS GOOD."

3. Lily of the Valley

Focusing Scripture

The spirit of God is in my nostrils.
(JOB 27:3)

To Think About

Lily of the valley, a small white flower with blossoms that hang like bells, is among the most fragrant of the spring wildflowers. (Hold up picture.) This flower has pointed to God for many people. Look at some of the things this flower has meant to people:

1. It is considered the sign of Christ's second coming. Why do you think this is so? Have you heard about the second coming of Christ? What do you think it means? Why would it be like this flower?

2. It is often called "ladder to heaven" and "Jacob's tears." (Read the story in Genesis 28:10-20.) Why would Jacob be crying? Look carefully at these blossoms. Can you see why someone might compare the blooms to angels going up to heaven? Have you ever thought of angels smelling good?

3. Some call this flower "Mary's tears." Legend says that when Mary cried at the cross, her tears turned into this flower. It is considered a symbol of purity, humility, sweetness, and renewed happiness.

Which of the three Bible illusions do you think the flower points to? Or is there another Bible story you would choose?

Activity

In this activity, we again search for wildflowers and use them as pointers, or signs, from God. Lily of the valley grows wild and also is cultivated in gardens. Examples may be obtained this way, but a better experience would be to discover it growing wild. It grows in large clusters, sometimes in extensive carpetlike colonies. Both the wildflower and the lily of the valley as we know it in our gardens may be found in woodland settings. Remind the class of your earlier discussion of what the flowers might symbolize.

Activity

It is difficult to describe a smell, an aroma, with words. Let's see if we can do it with this flower. What words would you use to describe the scent of a lily of the valley?

Look at the "Focusing Scripture" verse. What do you think it means?

After group discussion, end this experience by thanking God for the gift of smell, for the exquisite fragrance of this flower, and for all the wonderful aromas that add pleasure to our lives.

This activity might be experienced with the more common honeysuckle, or any other flower with a distinct, pleasant smell. The lemon or mint smell of crushed herb leaves might be used.

AND GOD SAID, "IT IS GOOD."

4. Water Lily

Focusing Scripture

> *"Can anything good come out of Nazareth?" . . . "Come and see."*
>
> (JOHN 1:46)

To Think About

Reflecting on the Flower: What is God's message to us from the water lily? (Show picture.) Once many years ago, someone looked at the spotlessly pure life of Jesus and, remembering the squalor of his hometown, asked, "Can anything good come out of Nazareth?"

Think about the history of our country and the history of your church. History is full of stories of heroes who came from very unimposing backgrounds. Which ones do you remember?

David was the greatest king in the Old Testament, yet he began life as a simple shepherd boy.

In I Chronicles 17:7, God says to David: "I took you from the pasture, from following the sheep, to be ruler over my people Israel," and David replies to God (in I Chronicles 17:16), "Who am I, O LORD God, and what is my house, that you have brought me thus far?"

In situations of unbelievable poverty and deprivation, love and kindness and goodness have blossomed. The movie *City of Joy* is a beautiful testimony of life lived fully and gloriously in the slums of Calcutta, in the midst of unbelievable conditions. The life and work of Mother Teresa is a true-life example. Deepest spirituality can be found in the midst of the most painful circumstances. This flower reminds us that life in God is so much more than place and surroundings!

Activity

Preparation for the Hike: Today we go looking for a water lily. These may be found in the city in an urban park or arboretum as well as in the woods. This lovely flower combines the innocently sweet fragrance of the lily of the valley and the secret in the roots of the bloodroot.

This flower, admired for its purity, when wild is found only in the rich, black mud of dead streams. Out of that fertile slime springs this spotless beauty. If possible, have the class gently feel both the silky softness of the pedals and the yukky glob of the roots.

AND GOD SAID, "IT IS GOOD."

5. Stop! And Discover Beauty

Focusing Scripture

> *Whatsoever things are lovely . . . think on these things.*
> (PHILIPPIANS 4:8 KJV)

To Think About

This experience will help the class become more aware of the beauty that surrounds us and encourage children to look upon things as good. Read to your class:

> With beauty before me,
> May I walk.
> With beauty behind me,
> May I walk.
> With beauty above me,
> May I walk.
> With beauty below me,
> May I walk.
> With beauty around me,
> May I walk.
> Wandering on a trail of beauty,
> Lively I walk.
> *NAVAJO NATION*

Activity

Play the game Running Water! Still Water! Stop! In a beautiful place outdoors, the class members line up some distance from the teacher, facing the teacher.

The children begin to run when the teacher calls: "Running water! Still water! Stop!" On "Stop," all the children stop and silently identify one beautiful thing they can see in front of them.

After a few seconds the teacher calls again: "Running Water! Still Water! Stop!"

This time the class stops at a spot closer to the teacher. The teacher says: "Using your sense of smell, hearing, sight, or touch, identify one beautiful thing behind you."

The game continues in this manner. On the third "Stop!" children identify a beautiful thing above them. The fourth time, they look down and identify something beautiful. On the fifth and final time, they stop and look to the right and left for something beautiful.

By now the children are close to the teacher, who instructs them to be seated. With paper and pencil, they write down the five beautiful things they have seen. The class shares answers. Did everyone observe the same beautiful things? How many different beautiful things were they able to discover?

Invite the children to shut their eyes and try to call up the images of those beautiful things. The teacher says: "Pretend your closed eyes are a blank movie screen. Project these images of beauty onto the screen. Know that you can recall these images of beauty any time you choose. Draw strength and comfort from these images. Sometimes in spiritual growth, our principal work is to look and see."

To Ponder

Here is the hard task. We shall never fully respect nature until we separate wild things from the notion of usability. Can you reflect on these beautiful things in their own right—just as they are? However innocent and harmless our use of them may be—think about this—why do we need to use them at all?

• Can we enjoy a flower without picking it?
• Can we respect a wild animal without wanting its skin or its meat?
• Can we admire river rocks without carting them away to our patios?

Is nature just for our use? What do you think?

AND GOD SAID, "IT IS GOOD."

6. Humor in Nature

Focusing Scripture

> *God's foolishness is wiser than human wisdom.*
> (I CORINTHIANS 1:25*a*)

To Think About

Nature seems to have a wonderful way of fitting whatever mood we may be in. It can speak to us whether we are silly and joyfully exuberant or somber and mourning. Today we are looking for the comic side of nature. Without drawing profound conclusions or probing deep mysteries, we celebrate the joys in nature.

In this activity, don't rob the class members of their own discoveries and imaginative ideas by over-teaching or over-directing. Don't emphasize identification. Asking "What is it?" too soon seems to inhibit rather than enhance imagination.

Activity

Instruct your class to go into the woods and find twigs and fallen tree branches (a piece of found art). Don't remove the twigs from living trees, but gather from fallen branches. Look for limbs with extending branches. Using your imagination, visualize critters from these twigs. Can you see a praying mantis, with tiny head and long, spindly legs? Perhaps you can see a crocodile with open jaws and ragged teeth. It is amazing what you can discover.

Returning to your classroom or outdoor area, scrape these wood pieces until the surface is smooth. Or leave the bark on, if that fits your design, and simply clean and remove any debris.

When your creations are prepared, paint the wood with bright paint. Add big eyes if appropriate. Use your imagination, the provocative piece of wood, and your particular vision to create a critter. Allow the paint to dry and then delight in the imaginative works of art. Laughter often accompanies this activity.

Reflect on the experience: Talk with the class about some of the living creatures in our world that are humorous looking. Ask: What is the funniest looking animal you have ever seen? Do you think God was having fun when these were being created? Do you think God laughed? There are animals like monkeys and crabs and giraffes which seem made to be laughed at. Think about God with a sense of humor, having fun.

AND GOD SAID, "IT IS GOOD."

7. Nature's Imperfections

Focusing Scripture

> *And when [Jesus] had said this, he showed them his hands and his feet.*
>
> (LUKE 24:40)

To Think About

Today we will go looking for imperfections in nature. Annie Dillard calls it "the flawed nature of perfection." We seek surprisingly endearing imperfections.

Here are two imperfections I have seen. Once the portions of the Appalachian Trail where I hike were used for grazing cattle, and barbed wire was strung around the fields. After this area was designated a national park, the barbed wire was removed, but on one tree a small bit remained. That little piece, sharp and barbed, cut harshly into the bark of the tree. Over the years, the tree had grown to encircle and encompass the ugly intruder, and the new growth was graceful and very beautiful.

On another part of the trail, a sign giving directions had been nailed onto a tree. Again, over the years, the tree had grown up and around and into the sign, making it a part of the tree itself.

I was reminded of the people I have known whose lives were struck by deep pain—situations they could not escape. Those persons also embraced the pain, just as the trees did, and their lives were more beautiful because of it. Children, too, experience woundedness and seek ways to grow stronger through their pain.

Nature kindly heals every wound; examples are all around us in the woods. A thousand little mosses and fungi cover the most unsightly objects, and they become radiant with beauty. I have even seen cans and other litter covered with vines and transformed.

Activity

Instruct the class to go looking for some imperfection, some intrusion. Insect infections on trees are called galls and some are very beautiful. Look for break points in trees, where a limb has been broken. If there is no break point, there is no transformation. Flowers whose leaves have been gnawed seem to glow more radiantly.

Give the class members ten minutes to go on their own into a designated nature area and look for imperfections that have been transformed into beauty. You might wish to set boundaries by hanging bandanas on trees beyond which the students cannot go. Look and ponder how nature heals.

Reflection on the Experience: On their return the class shares discoveries. Talk to the class about the "Focusing Scripture" passage. Jesus was identified by showing his wounds.

Ask the class to think about the wounds in their lives or in the lives of people they know. Some of us are physically wounded. We come to God with eyes that must be strengthened or repaired with a surgeon's skill. We come with ears augmented by hearing aids. We come with artificial hands or in a wheelchair or on crutches.

Some of us have spiritual wounds. We were forgotten or rejected or despised. Our first response may be anger and resentment. Why me? Feelings of hatred and self-loathing surface. We think about revenge. These feelings keep our wounds open.

Can we learn a lesson from nature? Can we embrace our wounds, claim our woundedness as our own unique way of being? Can we try to make something beautiful from our pain?

You may wish to tell your class about eagles' nests, which are great and beautiful and protected from all danger by their tremendous height. No marauder can menace the little ones. Yet the mother and father eagle have carefully woven thorns into the nest. These thorns are sharply turned inward so that the fledglings won't be too comfortable, but they will not be tempted to climb out. Are there thorns in your life? How can they work for good?

AND GOD SAID, "IT IS GOOD."

8. Mushroom Shapes

Focusing Scripture

> *Ask the plants of the earth, and they will teach you.*
>
> (JOB 12:8)

To Think About

How many different people do you know well? How many of a different race? A different heritage or tradition? How many with a different way of searching for God?

None of us can impose on others one pattern of becoming or being a disciple. All our views are too narrow. We need the experiences of other Christians. We cannot force people into molds, either in the way they become disciples of Jesus or in the way they practice their discipleship.

Just as the woods are far more beautiful when there are a variety of mushroom shapes, so is the Christian life.

Activity

In summer, after a rainy day, take the class on a mushroom hike. Many magical moments can be experienced. You may find a fairy ring of tiny mushrooms, a cluster of bells, a family of mushrooms around a stump, or delicately decorated fans. The colors and shadings may surprise you. You'll see white and beige and mahogany, brown, and orange. You might even see red, but you will never see a green mushroom. Though we traditionally think of mushrooms as being umbrella-shaped, there are actually many shapes. Nature has beautiful and ingenious designs. Some look like birdbaths, baseballs, rockets, or trumpets, but there are three common shapes: (1) the typical umbrella shape; (2) a club shape; and (3) a beefsteak shape that grows out from a tree.

On this hike, the concentration will be on the ability to observe shapes. Each student, with a small sketching pad and pencil, will search for a mushroom with an interesting or unusual shape and sketch it lightly. The emphasis is not on a finished product, but on the power of observation. You "see" more in nature when you take the time to draw what you find.

Back in the classroom, the students use waterproof India ink and go over the pencil lines of the mushroom shapes. After this has dried, each student is given a small brush and, using a mixture of one drop of ink in a tablespoon of water, brush over the pictures for an interesting effect. This will help them focus even more intently on shape.

AND GOD SAID, "IT IS GOOD."

9. Plants Point to Scripture

Focusing Scripture

> *The earth is full of the steadfast love of the LORD.*
> (PSALM 33:5*b*)

Reading Scripture alongside plant observation may open up a new way, both of viewing nature and of understanding Scripture. The three examples that follow might be experienced during the course of another hike, or may stand independently.

Activity

1. Take your Bible along on this excursion. You will be looking for a poisonous plant growing

alongside jewelweed. An interesting phenomenon to discover in nature is that healing plants often grow alongside poisonous ones.

The warning leaves of poison ivy and poison oak should be pointed out to your class: "Leaves of three, let it be." Stinging nettles are also plants to be avoided. The sting is as painful as it is short-lived.

But quite often, growing near these plants is the delicate and lovely touch-me-not, or jewelweed. After coming in contact with one of the dangerous plants, one can crush the touch-me-not (blossoms and leaves) and rub it on the affected area to take away the irritation.

To Think About

Read Mark 1:1-12, the story of the man who was healed with the help of his friends. Reflect on how humans depend upon and have a duty toward one another. Life, at its heart, has a mutual dependence. Consider: Are you a person who helps others, or hurts others? Think back over the past 24 hours for examples.

Activity

2. Look for a sassafras tree. This interesting tree has the unusual feature of different kinds of leaves growing on the same plant. Though different in shape and size, they exist quite healthily and happily together.

Draw a sassafras plant. Write the name of a different group in your church on each leaf shape. For example, the mitten-shaped leaf might be young children. Write "Jesus Christ" on the stem of your plant—the unifying force for all groups in the church.

To Think About

Read Romans 12:5: "We, who are many, are one body in Christ, and . . . we are members one of another." Looking at a sassafras is awakening us to the pervasiveness of division.

Activity

3. Find and consider the sunflower. Follow its daily path. The head or face of the flower faces the sun. It is fascinating to see a whole field of these flowers, all looking in the same direction—toward the sun.

To Think About

Read Jeremiah 2:27: "They have turned their backs to me, and not their faces."
When Jesus becomes the focal point of our lives, all our actions are determined by that focus.
Sunflowers remind us of that optimism of grace, which sets no limit to what God can do in human lives that are open to the fullness of God's love.
What other plants speak to you of God?

AND GOD SAID, "IT IS GOOD."

10. Trees

Focusing Scripture

Out of the ground the LORD *God made to grow every tree that is pleasant to the sight and good for food.*

(GENESIS 2:9)

To Think About

What do you hear in the trees? There is a story in our Old Testament about King David, the mighty warrior. As he was struggling to build the kingdom of Israel, he fought many battles with the Philistines, and before each battle he sought God's guidance.

Once the Philistines raided the valley of Raphaim, where the Israelites lived. David prayed to God, asking what he should do. The Lord replied: "When you hear the sound of marching in the tops of the balsam trees, then go out to battle; for God has gone out before you" (I Chron. 14:15).

Activities

1. The class chooses an outdoor area with at least six trees. The members of the class carefully study each tree. Say: Look at each tree thoroughly. Feel the bark. Walk around it. Try to determine how it is unique.

2. Name the trees. Forget all the scientific names and labels. Choose a name that reflects the disposition or character you see in each tree. For example: Strong One, Cheerful One, Graceful One, Independent One, Watchful One. Select the names thoughtfully, trying to capture the real essence of the tree. Some of the things we notice in trees are dignity, nobility, sturdiness, independence.

3. The class members share the names they have given the trees, explaining why the particular names were chosen. Are the names similar? The class then agrees on the best name for each tree. What pointers to God can you see in the tree and the name?

4. Have a naming ceremony. The class members circle each tree. One child says: "We name you (for example, Listening One), and we thank God for you. By this name we shall know you. We will remember your example when we need patience in our own lives."

The class members move to the next tree, circle it, and repeat the ceremony, with a different child and a different name. When all have been named, the members join in a time of silence, thinking about the uniqueness of each tree and listening to the sounds of the trees (their voices).

Encourage the class to keep in touch with these trees by visiting them at different seasons of the year, and noticing the changes.

5. Find a tree that has supple, low-hanging branches with leaves. Carefully bend down a bough of this tree. Have the class think of something for which they are thankful to God. Write the word gently on a leaf with a felt-tip pen. When all have written their thanksgivings, release the bough. Springing and dancing, it goes up and away. Imagine your prayers being flung upward to God.

Remember King David's story and listen to the grove of trees. What do you hear in the tops of trees?

6. Find a cluster of trees with upsweeping branches. It is fascinating to notice how the successive upward branchings conquer space. Unable to move any other way, trees reach upward.

Lie on your back under trees and look up. Watch for movement. Usually there is some movement at the very tops of trees, even on still days. Imagine the trees saying, "Lift up your hearts." Reply: "We lift them up unto the Lord."

Instruct the children to raise their arms like branches and repeat after you:

> Help us to grow beautiful
> Reaching up to you.
> (extend arms to the side)
> Help us to grow beautiful
> Reaching out to help others.

AND GOD SAID, "IT IS GOOD."

11. Walking in Snow

Focusing Scripture

> You show me the path of life.
> In your presence there is fullness of joy;
> in your right hand are pleasures forevermore.
>
> (PSALM 16:11)

To Think About

In this book many nature walks are suggested: spring wild-flower walks, summer-rain walks, autumn-leaf walks, night walks. Discovering God's mysteries through nature might also include a snow walk. Walking in places you have walked before, now transformed by the first snow, is an opening to new wonders.

This experience cannot be programmed. Each situation will be a unique adventure. Pick and choose from the following suggestions those that are appropriate for your class and what you encounter. Or create your own questions and activities.

Activity

The first snow excites us. Accept and accent this excitement in your classroom. Go outdoors as it begins and open all your senses to the experience. Tilt your head back and feel the snow falling on your face, piling up on your eyelashes. Catch it on your tongue.

Give each student a piece of black construction paper that has been in the freezer overnight. Catch snowflakes on the paper. The frozen paper will allow you to examine this unique, evaporating miracle a little longer. Notice how no two snowflakes are alike. How creative, beyond our imagining, is our God! As you catch the endlessly varying flakes on your paper, realize with awe the geometric order in this seemingly chaotic swirl.

When the snow covers the ground like a lumpy quilt, take a walk. Talk about how the individual snowflakes have merged—their individual detailed structures have disappeared and an even floor of snow is now beneath us.

On this fresh snow surface, look for animal tracks. If you look closely, you may see hundreds of footprints and wingprints. Can you recognize what made them? It's as if a night letter had been written in this snow.

If you find a particularly interesting set of tracks, stop and let the students make up a story to explain the tracks. What was happening here? Later, back in the classroom, students may want to draw and create a story using only tracks. It's fun to share these stories and see whether the other students can follow the track story.

As you continue to walk, look at the trees in winter snow—nothing is more beautiful. Fluffy snow may have collected in heavy clumps on evergreens and, with unexpected release, may fall plop on your head. Reflect with your class on how a weak branch might snap under the weight of snow. How can one little snowflake, which weighs nothing, be the final breaking point? Compare it with "the straw that broke the camel's back." What do you think this means?

Ask whether anyone can give an example from their own life of a similar situation? When was one little incident the breaking point—when you had taken all you could and one little thing set you off? Can you think of an example from the Bible? What about when Jesus turned over the tables of the moneychangers in the temple?

Look for trees and plants that curl up their leaves tightly when it's cold—for example, laurel leaves. The colder it is, the more tightly they close.

You may discover snow on vertical surfaces. Snow, moving on air that has collided with a stationary object, may immediately freeze there. Ask the class members whether they can tell from this which way the wind is blowing. Use this to talk about wind and its invisible power. Ask why the Spirit of God is often compared to wind. Looking in the distance to a mountain ridge, you might see snow that seems to be dancing, blown upward by the wind.

Look at the beautiful patterns formed by bare tree limbs softened with snow. Later, you may want to try to capture this pattern with *scherenschnitt.* This is a folk art which cuts the design of the tree branch from black paper with small, sharp scissors. An art teacher or parent could help with this.

Stand very still and listen to the muffled silence of snow. It's as if your ears are stuffed with cotton. With the class, try to capture this muffled sound. Create a snow chorus. For example:

> rustle-hush
> rustle-hush
> rustle-hush
> Shhhhhhh

What sounds can they suggest? Try putting the sounds together.

Now instruct the students to try to become part of this scene. Look all around at the new wonders and signs God gives through this snow-covered world. Tell the class members to think deeply, as they look and absorb, about these words from St. Francis: "At all times, preach the gospel and, if you must, use words." How many ways, in this snow-covered world, is the gospel being preached without words?

AND GOD SAID, "IT IS GOOD."

MORNING

Discovering Beauty

Teach me your way, O LORD,
that I may walk in your truth.
(PSALM 86:11)

The spirit of God
is in my nostrils.
(JOB 27:3b)

Whatsover things are lovely . . .
think on these things.
(PHILIPPIANS 4:8 KJV)

God's foolishness is
wiser than human wisdom.
(I CORINTHIANS 1:25)

Ask the plants of the earth,
and they will teach you.
(JOB 12:8)

Out of the ground the Lord God made
to grow every tree that is pleasant to
the sight and good for food.
(GENESIS 2:9)

Chapter Three

NOON

A Time to Reflect

▬ ▬ ▬ ▬ ▬ ▬ ▬ ▬ ▬ ▬ ▬ ▬ ▬ ▬ ▬ ▬ ▬ ▬

In the middle of the day—high noon—we pause. We have awakened. We have explored and discovered beauty. Now we pause to reflect, to seek nourishment, to stand back and look at what we have been doing. We try to gain some understanding and to befriend the discoveries we have made.

We listen to stories and songs. We ponder their meaning for us. We make use of art activities to lead us to deeper understanding. This is a quiet time for loving and leading children into the wonder of God and God's creation.

Here is a mystery: Jesus, the Christ, the Word we know as Jesus, is like the heartbeat of the entire created universe—beating out its meaning. If we desire to understand the universe, we are enabled to do so only through the Christ. The heart of the universe is personal. The heart of the universe is the personal love of God. This very moment is trembling with the possibilities of God's love and presence.

Listening, watching, and drawing conclusions, we seek a different angle of vision.

The format of this chapter varies from the previous ones as we mingle pondering and activities. Stretching our minds to new thoughts is emphasized. Before attempting an activity, read through the entire experience, since leader's instructions are interspersed with activities and pondering.

Do these experiences at your own pace, being sensitive to how much your class is grasping. These activities take place indoors, and at the end of each, we become quiet, reflective, and receptive. Nature is deep. We will never exhaust its meaning.

1. The Lost Song

Focusing Scripture

> *I will sing to the LORD as long as I live;*
> *I will sing praise to my God while I have being.*
>
> (PSALM 104:33)

To Think About

Seated in a quiet place, with a lovely outdoor view if possible, the teacher tells this story in her or his own words.

This story comes from the Bambuti, a nomadic pygmy tribe in the Congo's Ituri forest.

Once a Bambuti boy was walking in the rain forest, where towering trees reach 150 feet, where tangled creepers and vines press down, where constant movement lets you see plants growing. In this forest, he heard a beautiful song that he had never heard before. Following the sound, he came upon a rare and beautiful bird. The bird told the boy it was hungry. The boy rushed back to tell his father, but his father said, "Why waste food on a strange bird?"

For the next two days, the boy again heard the beautiful song, met the rare bird, and was asked for food. Each time, the boy rushed back to his father to beg for food, and each time, the father refused and became more and more angry.

Finally the father ordered the boy to leave, and when the boy was gone, the father found the bird and killed it. And the beautiful song died. No other living thing could repeat it. The father killed the song when he killed the bird. He robbed the forest of some of its beauty.

Activity

Teacher: Using your imagination, draw the rare and beautiful bird in this story. Color the bird in the most beautiful, imaginative way you can. Try putting colors together in new combinations. Use origami paper with its beautiful colors, and cut it into strips and patterns to decorate your bird.

In Harry Chapin's song "Flowers Are Red," a stern teacher says to a five-year-old child: "Flowers are red. Green leaves are green." The teacher thought that flowers should be colored the way they really look.

But the little boy sees the colors of the rainbow and the morning sun within the flower. The point of this activity is to affirm that seeing.

To Think About

Reflect on all the plants and animals that are no longer in our world—lost forever—from giant dinosaurs to tiny orchids.

Can the class name any animals now on the endangered species list? A broad question can start children thinking about a topic and give them a chance to tell what they already know. (Possible answers include the whooping crane, the big ivory-billed woodpecker, little key deer.)

The beauty of the world and its ability to sustain a vast multitude of species cannot be taken for granted.

What are some lost sounds in the world? Invite the children to close their eyes. Say:

Try to imagine the sound of a bird's song as it sings to God. (silence)

Try to imagine the sound of wind through trees, singing to God. (silence)

Hum silently to yourself your special song to God. There is deep inner music in each of us. (silence)

Now, learn this Bible verse with me (class repeats after teacher):

> I will sing to the LORD as long as I live;
> I will sing praise to my God while I have being.

> (Psalm 104:33)

AND GOD SAID, "IT IS GOOD."

2. Green Chaos

Focusing Scripture

"Can you see anything?" And the man looked up and said, "I can see people, but they look like trees, walking."

(MARK 8:23c, 24)

To Think About

Look at the woods in the distance—trees, shrubs, vines, merged together. It is difficult to isolate a separate boundary for each shade. It looks like green chaos. Scan the visual space. How many different shades of green can you see? All nature seen this way seems chaotic—a vast expanse of weeds, brush, thickets.

Identify at least five different shades of green. Paint-sample cards could be used for matching colors.

Activity

Cut a small colored picture about one-inch square out of a magazine. Choose a picture with many shades of green. Paste the picture in the center of a sheet of paper. Using colored pencils in a variety of green tones, work out from the edges of the picture, trying to match the color tones exactly. Flare the colors out in a sun burst. Now exchange pictures. Can each person find the other's camouflaged square?

This chaos that we see in nature is present also in our lives. So many things crowd into every moment. Past memories and present perceptions, times and places, unique talents and family expectations. At any moment, we are a jumble of all these.

None of us is all that we might be. Hidden within us may be potential that is lost in the chaos.

Look at the person whose paper you have examined for the camouflaged square. It might be someone you know well or a stranger. What hidden potential might be in that person? Based on what you see in or about that person, any hints or clues you may have picked up, write a great hidden potential that you think he or she might have. Share with each other the potentials and the reason for your choice. Did this hidden potential come as a surprise to that person, or did the person suspect that he or she had this potential?

To Ponder

We learn from nature that a portion of territory which the eye can comprehend is only a single view. There is more—much more.

Read the entire Gospel story in Mark 8:22-26. "What do you see?" our Lord asked. "Green chaos." Jesus touches us and says "Look again." If once we could see the trees clearly, and then could identify with each person walking, we might see more—far more.

Become quiet and reflect on these things.

AND GOD SAID, "IT IS GOOD."

3. How Our Environment Affects Us

Focusing Scripture

> *Where can I go from your spirit?*
> *Or where can I flee from your presence?*
>
> (PSALM 139:7)

To Think About

Nature has a subtle but profound effect on us—more than we perhaps realize. The nature that surrounds us affects our view of the world. I live in an area with lots of trees and mountains. A friend, growing up in the plains, says that this area makes her feel as if the trees and mountains are smothering her, threatening her. To me, they are embracing arms, sheltering me.

Jill Ker Conway, in *The Road from Coorain,* says that the environment in which we grow up affects both our worldview and predominant myths.

The unpredictability of rain in some areas shapes the conversation of the people there. They discuss events in terms of their probability of occurrence, avoiding any assumption that an event will surely happen.

Some find the ocean cold and frightening; others find it a great reservoir of strength.

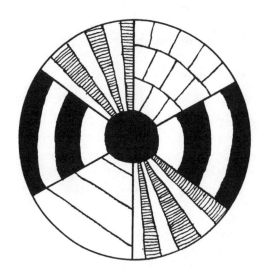

Activity

Draw a natural plot, a landscape, of the area where you grew up. In the very center of your environmental plot, draw a circle to represent God.

Invite the class to share their experiences of living in various places. Discuss how environment may have shaped their beliefs:

1. As a result of your environment, do you see the world as threatening? fearful? beautiful? harsh?

2. Swap your picture with someone from a different environment. Try to imagine living in a

completely different environment, perhaps much hotter or colder. How would this affect your view of the world and your image of God?

3. What type of environment means "home" to you? Can you explain your choice? Each of us harbors a homeland, a landscape we naturally prefer. What type of environment makes you feel most secure and at home?

4. Think of biblical characters. How did the environment affect them? For example:

A. If you had spent your life as a follower of Moses, wandering through the desert, what would be most important in your life? How would you picture God?

B. If you had been on the ark with Noah, what would be most important in your life? How would you picture God?

To Ponder

Whatever our environment, our home base, God is at the center. Become quiet. Ask God to give you understanding.

AND GOD SAID, "IT IS GOOD."

4. Mandalas of Beauty

Focusing Scripture

> *For everything there is a season, and a time for every matter under heaven.*
> (ECCLESIASTES 3:1)

To Think About

The point of this activity is to make students aware of a different view of life—a life with more joy and awareness, with heightened consciousness. We attempt to do this by feeling our way into the seasons of the year with the use of three tools: color, words, and our bodies. The colors represent the intrinsic form of the season. The words capture its feeling, and our bodies affirm that we are a part.

Activity

Give each student a piece of poster paper with a large circle drawn on it. They are instructed, beginning at 12 noon, to write, clockwise on the outside line of the circle, words that capture all the good senses, feelings, and images of spring. They may be single words, phrases, or sentences. Use colored pencils with the colors you associate with the season.

Using other sheets of poster paper, make circle poems for summer, autumn, and winter. Encourage the students to get in touch with their feelings for each season: the budding and newness of spring; the flowering and fruiting of summer; drying plant life in autumn; and the stark beauty of winter.

When all have finished, the class becomes the poem. Standing in a circle, we realize we are dwelling in the presence of Mystery. The author of one poem assigns each student a word from that poem. (If there are too many students, the extra ones sit down and softly chant as an ostinato, "Spring, Summer, Winter, Fall." If there are too few, each student can be assigned more than one word.)

The class members perform the poem by saying their given word(s) in correct order around the circle. The next student author directs the class in performing his or her poem in a similar manner. If all the seasons are performed, group all spring poems together, all summer poems, and so on.

The students get a feel for the season with freshness, a great givingness, and joy. Their own feelings are expressed, and their appreciation is expanded as they listen to other feelings.

Now create an art piece from the circle poem. Instruct the students: "In the empty space within your circle, find a center point. Create a design, using squares and triangles that radiate from this center. No two designs should be alike."

Color the design. Let the colors you choose represent the season of the poem. For example: Spring might be yellow and blue; summer, red and gold; autumn, brown and orange; winter, white and silver.

The posters, with their appropriate colors, now become art work for your room.

To Ponder

Sit quietly, reflecting on the colors and shapes and words. Seek inner wisdom. Notice the influence of the colors on one another. What color is at the center? What colors touch? Reflect on the heart of the Mystery that resides at the center of everything that is—the still point of the turning world.

AND GOD SAID, "IT IS GOOD."

5. Abundance in Nature

Focusing Scripture

> For [God] gives the Spirit without measure.
>
> (JOHN 3:34*b*)

To Think About

There is no "enough" to nature. It is a feast—an immense extravagance—all giving, giving, giving.

Compare your life to the giving . . . giving . . . giving of God. Do you like to accumulate things? Think about your closet at home. Can you recall any toy or game or piece of clothing you really, really wanted, but then after you received it, it sort of went into the closet and was forgotten? Have you ever collected something you really didn't like or want, but kept on collecting more of it anyway?

Think again about how freely God gives in nature. Compare yourself. Is it hard for you to give? Is it hard for you to share?

Ponder the opening sentence: There is no "enough" to nature.

Think about a gift you could give to another person. Ask God to give you an open, sharing, spirit.

Think of something beautiful you could give to God.

Think about Jesus. The cross is the ultimate example of giving.

Then learn the song on pages 52-53.

Activity:

Say: "You have two minutes to list all the animals you can think of. Write as fast as you can."

After two minutes, ask: "Who has the most?" Read that list. What animals on the other lists were not included in the first list? How many animals did the group come up with in two minutes?

AND GOD SAID, "IT IS GOOD."

6. Imitations

Focusing Scripture

> *I am the true vine, and my Father is the vinegrower.*
>
> (JOHN 15:1)

To Think About

It's fun to draw pictures of nature and create things from nature, but nothing we create can ever begin to compare with God's creation.

> Our God is in the heavens;
>   he does whatever he pleases.
> Their idols are silver and gold,
>   the work of human hands.
> They have mouths, but do not speak;
>   eyes, but do not see.
> They have ears, but do not hear;
>   noses, but do not smell.
> They have hands, but do not feel;
>   feet, but do not walk;
>   they make no sound in their throats.
> Those who make them are like them;
>   so are all who trust in them.
>
> (PSALM 115:3-8)

Continued on page 54.

Wisely Made!
(Psalm 104:24)

Lord, you have made so ma-ny things! How wise-ly you made them, made them all! The earth is filled, filled with your crea - tures. How wise - ly you made them, made them all!

WORDS: James Ritchie (adapted from Psalm 104:24, *Good News Bible*)
MUSIC: James Ritchie
ARRANGEMENT: Timothy Edmonds

8ba

Activity

1. With a box of stars and a sheet of black or dark blue construction paper, arrange the stars on the paper as beautifully as you can. Then go outside on a dark night and look at the stars overhead (or remember such an occasion). What was missing in your picture?

2. Pass around a commercial product advertised as having a pine smell. Then go into a pine thicket and smell (or remember such an occasion). What was missing?

3. Pass around some artificial flowers (silk or plastic). Arrange them in a vase. Then go out and look at flowers in a garden (or remember such an occasion). What was missing?

4. Obtain a small square of grasslike indoor/outdoor carpet or a grass-design welcome mat. Sit on it. Then go outside and sit in real grass (or remember such an occasion). What was missing?

5. Make masks for yourselves out of paper plates. Make them as beautiful as you can. Look at one another with the masks on. Then remove them. What was missing?

Say in your own words: All our knowledge and the best techniques we can develop are no more than replicas or imitations. What is irreplaceable is the Spirit of God present in all created things. Why should we settle for any god except our wondrous Creator God, known to us in Jesus?

I saw a banner in a church: "God is as close to us as we can risk being close to our real selves." We also are creations of God.

Are we real or imitation?

Why do some people imitate other people?

Write down some ways you have imitated others, instead of being yourself. Try to understand a little better the one and only, original, no-imitation you, and all the good things God has done for you. Like things in nature, the imitation is never as good as the original.

To Ponder

Jesus said, "I am the true vine." Think about the Jesus we only read about in books. We can know the real Jesus, and once we do, we recognize the great difference.

How can you try to know the real Jesus? Become quiet, and ask God to give you understanding.

AND GOD SAID, "IT IS GOOD."

7. Break Time

Focusing Scripture

> *Let everything that breathes praise the LORD!*
> *Praise the LORD!*
>
> (PSALM 150:6)

To Think About

It is relaxing and refreshing to play games together. If your class needs a break from heavy pondering, or if you wish to promote fellowship in the group or give an outlet to some pent-up energy, or if you just want to have some fun, try one of these games.

Activity

GAME 1: HOOTS AND ROARS

Divide the class into circles of six to eight persons. Someone in each circle makes a sound from nature (animal sounds, reptile sounds, water sounds, bird sounds, wind sounds). The next person repeats that sound and adds another, and so on around the circle. Anyone who forgets a sound or gets them confused or cannot think of another sound must sit in the middle of the circle. Game continues until only one person is left. This is a noisy, lively game. Afterward, the entire group joins in a "Howllelujah Chorus," making appropriate sounds after each sentence.

PRAISE GOD, ALL BIRDS OF THE AIR!
    Sounds
PRAISE GOD, ALL FISH OF THE SEA!
    Sounds
PRAISE GOD, ALL BEASTS OF THE JUNGLE!
    Sounds
PRAISE GOD, ALL ANIMALS OF THE FARM!
    Sounds
PRAISE GOD, ALL FROGS, TOADS, LIZARDS, AND SNAKES!
    Sounds
PRAISE GOD, ALL EARTHQUAKES AND VOLCANO BLASTS!
    Sounds
PRAISE GOD, ALL WINDS THAT BLOW ACROSS THE EARTH—
TORNADOES, HURRICANES, AND GENTLE BREEZES!
    Sounds
PRAISE GOD, ALL OCEANS, LAKES, AND STREAMS!
    Sounds
PRAISE GOD, ALL QUIET THINGS—THE SILENCE OF THE NIGHT—
THE STILLNESS OF THE DAWN.
    Sounds
LET EVERY LIVING THING PRAISE GOD!
    Sounds from all of God's creation.
LET US WORSHIP THE GOD OF CREATION!
(Prepared by Bill Peterson, Executive Director of the Montreat Conference Center, for the 1991 Christian Education Conference, Montreat, N. Car.)

GAME 2: THE UNICORN LOSES ITS HORN

A unicorn is an imaginary animal with one horn in the middle of its forehead. Without the horn, the unicorn is powerless.

The players wad up sheets of paper, tilt their heads back, and place the wads of paper on their foreheads (unicorn horns). To peppy music, all the unicorns walk around the room, balancing their horns. If a horn should fall off, that player must freeze and not move. That player can be rescued only if another player will reach down, get the fallen horn, and replace it. The rescuing player may hold his own paper horn while picking up the frozen player's horn. This is the only time hands can be used to steady a horn.

If the class is young or having too much trouble balancing, the horn may be placed on top of the head rather than on the forehead.

GAME 3: SPIDERWEB

Give every two players a ball of yarn of a color different from those given to other pairs of players. Clothespin one end of each ball of yarn to a stationary object. At a given signal, one player of each color unwinds the yarn—in and out and roundabout various objects and over and under the other players' yarn—until the whole ball is unwound or time is called. When the leader gives another signal, the second player on each team must untangle the giant spiderweb.

GAME 4: RHYMING RIDDLES (THIS ONE IS FOR THE BIRDS!)

Divide the class into teams. Give each team a Scripture passage about a bird. After reading their passage, each team must make up a rhyming riddle about their particular bird. Then the other teams try to guess what bird it is.
(Scripture passages about birds: I Kings 17:6; Genesis 8:11; Matthew 26:75; Numbers 11:31; Matthew 10:29; Luke 2:24; I Samuel 26:20; Matthew 23:37; Daniel 7:4; Isaiah 34:14)

GAME 5: ANIMAL, VEGETABLE, MINERAL

"It" chooses a nature object visible in a given area. The group can ask only 20 questions. "It" can answer only "Yes" or "No." The group has three guesses to come up with the correct answer before the 20 questions are used up.

AND GOD SAID, "IT IS GOOD."

8. Birds in Flight

Focusing Scripture

> *As an eagle . . . spreads its wings, takes them up,*
> *and bears them aloft on its pinions,*
> *the LORD alone guided him.*
> (DEUTERONOMY 32:11-12*a*)

To Think About

Look at the sky and try to discover birds in flight. There is something about this experience that gladdens the heart. You might see birds gliding like a work of art, music in flight. You might see birds in formation. Look for birds flying together. Look for birds flying alone.

Have you ever noticed the awkward flapping flight of a crow? It seems heavy and ponderous. By contrast, have you ever seen an eagle in flight? There is a graceful dipping and soaring, moving on air currents—at times motionless, at other times with powerful upward strokes of grace and beauty.

Think about your own life. Recall trying too hard to do something that did not suit you. It is a lot of work to do what we are not cut out to do, something we really do not want to do at all. We are like that flopping old crow.

Now recall doing something that seemed effortless and right for you. It's like the eagle flight. You find your thermal and wing it from there. This can be a great test for discovering what we are meant to do.

Ask God to speak to you through birds in flight, to guide you and help you understand what you were meant to be and do. An auspicious occasion (from the Latin word *avis*) is one in which the birds are seen to fly in the right direction. Are you flying in the right direction for your life?

Activity

Read aloud the hymn "On Eagle's Wings."

SEATED EAGLE DANCE

Caller: All join hands and circle hands around.
  (And God will raise you up on eagle's wings,)
Caller: Now circle joined hands the other way round.
  (bear you on the breath of dawn,)
Caller: Sway separated hands in front of you—fingers open.
  (make you to shine like the sun,)
Caller: Join hands again, raise arms, and sway hands overhead.
  (and hold you in the palm of God's hand.)
("On Eagle's Wings," © 1979, 1991, New Dawn Music, P.O. Box 13248, Portland, OR 97213. All rights reserved. Used with permission.)

AND GOD SAID, "IT IS GOOD."

9. God of the Sparrow

Focusing Scripture

> *Remember the wonderful works he has done,*
>   *his miracles.*
>
> (I CHRONICLES 16:12)

To Think About

Great power is released when we recall Bible stories and images from our own experiences, and let these two images meld together. The Bible stories become stories about us, and we realize that all of life is holy.

In the hymn "God of the Sparrow," each phrase of the hymn touches our memory of a biblical event. From deep within us, they raise images. The first two verses, particularly, pick up biblical images from nature, to put us in touch with God. We remember the Bible story and, with ringing truth, it connects with our stories.

Activity

1. Look at the first phrase of the hymn: "God of the sparrow." Recall Jesus' words that not a sparrow falls to the earth but his Father knows. Have you ever heard the line from the old gospel hymn, "His eye is on the sparrow and I know he watches me"?

Now recall the last time you saw a sparrow—a tiny brown bird. Where were you? What was happening? Let the two images merge. Our God is a God of small things.

2. Look at the next phrase: "God of the whale." Call to mind our great biblical whale story and Jonah, and its ringing message, "You cannot run away from God."

Now recall any personal experience you have had with a giant sea creature. It may be only recalling a picture, or perhaps you have glimpsed an actual whale. Let these two images merge. Our God is a God of great things.

3. "God of the swirling stars." Recall our creation stories, when the light was separated from the dark. The sun and moon appeared in this great void, and the stars twirled and danced. Now recall any experience you have had with space. Have you ever looked through a telescope? Attended a planetarium show? Have you read of quasars and black holes in space and star quakes? Let the images merge. Our God is not afraid of boundless space.

As we recall these images, we cry, "Awe." We cry, "Praise." Look at the second verse:

1. "God of the earthquake." Recall the biblical earthquake stories. Remember that the veil of the temple was rent when Jesus was crucified. Now, bring up any personal experiences you have had with earthquakes. If you have never experienced the ground trembling beneath you, you have seen on television the results of this power. Let the images merge.

2. "God of the storm." There are many storm stories in the Bible. We remember that Jesus was asleep in a boat with his disciples on the Sea of Galilee when a sudden, violent storm arose. All of us have experienced some sort of storm, if not the overwhelming vortex of a hurricane or tornado, at least the rumbling surges of a thunderstorm. Let the images merge.

3. "God of the trumpet blast." Our biblical stories vibrate to this sound—Joshua at Jericho, Gabriel at the second coming of Christ. Now remember the last time you heard the sound of brass instruments. Recall the particular timber of that sound. Let the images merge.

When we are in the presence of God in nature, we are sometimes fearful. And we cry, "Woe," and we plead, "Save."

Now add to your images the dimension of music. Sing these two verses.

The class might be interested in recalling other Bible stories, or images from the other verses. The last verse is a powerful affirmation, when we are no longer creatures but children, and our response is "joy," and our word is "home."

("God of the Sparrow," words copyright © 1983, Jaroslav Vajda. Used by permission.)

AND GOD SAID, "IT IS GOOD."

10. Nature in the Easter Story

Focusing Scripture

Now there was a garden in the place where he was crucified.
(JOHN 19:41)

To Think About

The central story of our faith took place in a garden. As a time of personal devotion, and to remind yourself of their content, read the following four passages: Matthew 28:1-10; Mark 16:1-8; Luke 24:1-12; John 20:1-10.

Activity

Step 1: Divide the class into four groups. Give each group one of the above Scripture passages to read. Instruct the groups to identify all the nature objects in the Scripture selection.

Step 2: Groups share answers.

Step 3: Entire group reads the story in John 20:11-18. (Mary mistakes Jesus for the gardener.)

Step 4: Each student chooses one nature object mentioned in any of the stories and paints or draws that object. No peeping to see what another student chooses.

Step 5: On a long sheet of mural paper, draw the outline of a cave with an open entrance. Now the students cut out their nature objects and glue them on the mural paper.

The result of the different nature objects in different sizes and shapes creates a surrealistic view of Easter. In the sky, for example, there may be several suns and a lightning flash.

Step 6: With crayons, sketch in some background (blue for sky, green for grass) to complete the mural.

Stand back and look at the work. Open your mind to new understandings about this miraculous event.

AND GOD SAID, "IT IS GOOD."

NOON

A Time to Reflect

Where can I go from your spirit?
Or where can I flee from your presence?
(PSALM 139:7)

For everything there is a season,
and a time for every matter under heaven.
(ECCLESIASTES 3:1)

I am the true vine, and my Father is the
vinegrower.
(JOHN 15:1)

Remember the wonderful works he has done,
his miracles.
(I CHRONICLES 16:12)

As an eagle . . .
spreads its wings, takes them up,
and bears them aloft on its pinions,
the LORD alone guided him.
(DEUTERONOMY 32:11)

Let everything that breathes praise the LORD!
Praise the LORD!
(PSALM 150:6)

Chapter Four

AFTERNOON

Behold!

━ ━

We have awakened. We have gone forth to discover beauty. We have remained still and reflected. Our spiritual life, like the movement of a day or the years of our lives, does not stop. We do not reach a plateau and stay there. Throughout our lives, experiences cause us to rethink, to seek new discoveries that will lead to new understandings. If our spirituality is a living one, each experience will occur at a deeper level.

In this section, we set forth again to discover the clear manifestations of God's love in the richness of nature. We look now at the animals that share this world with us. We look at rocks, long a biblical metaphor. We ponder water—what it means in the physical and spiritual sense. The materials of nature keep us in touch with reality. The spiritual images that these materials evoke put us in touch with God. We seek this link, this connection between our images and nature's material.

You may have seen the puzzle picture which, if you look at it one way, seems to be two profiles. If you look at it another way, it seems to be a vase. When we look at nature, we also can see a double image. We see the thing itself, and we perceive behind the world and in the world the presence of Jesus. Jesus said, "I am the light of the world. I am the resurrection." Jesus represents himself as God's gift to us. Once we realize who Jesus is, we have a new perspective on the whole world, and then our "seeing" directs our actions. Our approach is awe and reverence.

In this section, we seek the double vision. We will go both indoors and outdoors to make discoveries. Outdoors we will view lakes, rocks and other inanimate objects, and play some lively games. We will follow a stream and hike in the rain. In the classroom, we will use art to understand animals and rocks in a new way. And again we will come up against new puzzlements for our understandings.

1. Inanimate Beauty

Focusing Scripture

> *I believe that I shall see the goodness of the* Lord
> *in the land of the living.*
>
> (PSALM 27:13)

To Think About

Ponder together Genesis 2:5-7. In this story, the creating of everything except humans was accomplished when God spoke a word—"And it was so." But in verse 2:7, we read that the first human was created when God breathed into his nostrils the breath of life. The breath of God gives us life.

We are continually being created. We can change, and we can hope. We are not yet all that we can be, no matter what our age or condition.

Activity

In an outdoor area if possible, the class goes on a scavenger hunt to find a thing of inanimate beauty (something beautiful that has never lived).

Say that each class member is to find a beautiful, lifeless thing in nature—something that never had life—for example, a snowflake or a lovely frost pattern formed on a windowpane. Some people call that beautiful pattern "frost flower." It does look like a flower, though it never had life. Someone may find a spiderweb or bird nest. Look for any beautiful thing in nature that never had life. Set boundaries and a time limit.

When the time is up and the class members have returned, talk about what they discovered. Recall with them the story of Pinnochio, the puppet who came to life when he began to have feelings. Not being able to feel emotions is a terrible loss. Talk with the class about how inanimate things may be beautiful, but they can never change. They cannot even know that they are beautiful. Inanimate things cannot hope or feel.

Invite the class members to write an imaginary story in which the beautiful lifeless thing they discovered comes alive. What would it see? What would it think? Because of its size and location, what human characteristics would you give it?

Share the stories. Was there hoping and feeling? Was the object glad to be alive?

AND GOD SAID, "IT IS GOOD."

2. Sparkling Mountains and Butterflies

Focusing Scripture

> *Its stones are the place of sapphires,*
> *and its dust contains gold.*
>
> (JOB 28:6)

To Think About

From the Ojibway Native American heritage comes this story:

The Creator made mountains, cliffs, precipices, and escarpments. Looking at them, the Creator thought these massive rocks were too imposing and dark and gray and dreary. And so the Creator fashioned pebbles of brilliant hues of white, crimson, green, blue, yellow, amber, and azure, and flung them against the mountains and cliffs. Immediately, the rocks and mountains began to sparkle and shimmer. The people became inordinately fond of these colored mountains, but the young children began to cry. There was nothing down on their level to bring them joy and happiness. And so the Creator took some of the colored pebbles and threw them to the wind. Immediately, the stones changed into butterflies, fluttering and dancing around the children. And they became the spirit of children's play.

(Basil Johnson, *Ojibway Heritage* [Columbia University Press, 1976])

Activity

Illustrate this lovely myth. On the top half of a piece of manila art paper, draw and color stark gray cliffs. On the bottom half, draw a meadow and outline butterflies in the meadow. Dab droplets of glue all over the mountains and butterflies. Then shake glitter (in silver, gold, red, etc.) onto the picture. Carefully shake off the excess glitter. The glitter that remains on the paper will give you a picture of shimmering mountains and sparkling butterflies.

Activity

If you live in a region where it is possible to collect small colorful rocks, or an urban area where there are rock shops or rock shows, make an adventure of discovering colorful pebbles. Invite the children to bring in small colorful rocks they find. Display each rock individually in a section of an egg carton. In this way, children will become aware of God's sparkling surprises in common pebbles.

The colors in the stones may be brought out with a light coating of cooking oil. Many rock enthusiasts have small rock polishers and may be willing to demonstrate its use and share their rock collection.

Tell the children that we can be like sparkling pebbles in the world. We can do small deeds of kindness that will brighten the world around us. Think of some shining pebbles you can give: a smile, a kind word. These are gems of beauty that children bring forth in others with their acts of thoughtfulness. Be a shinning pebble today.

AND GOD SAID, "IT IS GOOD."

3. Like a Rock

Focusing Scripture

> Be a rock of refuge for me,
>   a strong fortress to save me.
> You are indeed my rock and my fortress;
>   for your name's sake lead me and guide me.
>
> (PSALM 31:2b-3)

To Think About

Today children are called upon to be strong. For some, traditional support is gone. Perhaps a child is a latch-key child, home alone in the afternoon. Perhaps a child is from a one-parent family and is expected to carry adult burdens. Children often live away from grandparents and other relatives. The nature image of a rock can help.

Activity

Go with the class to discover rocks. Find an interesting large rock or boulder. Walk around it. Study it. Where is it located? How did it get there? Hunch your body into the shape of the rock. Place your hand on it. What is its temperature? Get the picture and feel of this rock firmly in your mind.

MEDITATION

Invite the class to sit quietly as you direct their thinking:

The thing we notice most about a boulder is its strength and endurance. Ask God to teach you how to be strong inside—to have inner strength. Think about the following situations. Then think about the rock. Go back and forth in your mind.

- You are tempted to give up on some homework that is too difficult. Picture the rock.
- You are watching more TV than you know is good for you. Picture the rock.
- Your friends are taunting and teasing a person who is different. Think about the rock. You can stand up against the crowd. You are strong.
- You want to go and play, but you have jobs to finish. Picture the rock.
- You must wait a long time for something you want. Picture the rock.
- You do not learn as easily and quickly as some of your friends. Picture the rock.
- You have physically handicapping traits. Think about the rock.
- You are tempted to try drugs. Picture the rock.
- You are surrounded by people who fuss and argue. Picture the rock.
  Call yourself "Rocky," "Stony," or "Flint." You can endure.

You are strong. By carrying with you the strong nature image of a large rock or boulder and remembering the Bible verse, you can face life's challenges with fortitude and courage.

Sometimes pain is just to be lived through. We meet it and survive. Remember the rock. Imagine it in rain storms and ice storms and snow storms and blistering heat. Be strong—like a rock.

Prayer: Children form a circle. The leader sets an atmosphere of reverence. A rock is passed around the circle. As the rock is held, each child is invited to say a prayer, either silently or aloud, asking for strength. As the rock is passed on, each child says a blessing to the next person: "_____, may you be strong in the Lord." The leader closes with Ephesians 6:10: "Be strong in the Lord and in the strength of his power."

AND GOD SAID, "IT IS GOOD."

4. Animal Worlds

Focusing Scripture

> *But ask the animals, and they will teach you;*
> *the birds of the air, and they will tell you.*
>
> (JOB 12:7)

To Think About

Let us consider now the wonderful world of animals, the other living creatures who inhabit the world with us. We are drawn to animals, not just because they are lively or pretty, but because we can think through them. Many times we use animals to wrap our ideas in visible form. For example:

> We are busy as beavers.
> Mad as hornets.
> Happy as larks.

Cross as bears.
Can you think of other examples?

There is great joy in recognizing and understanding life outside of one's own form. Animal behavior gives us greater understanding of human behavior. To know the thousands upon thousands of creatures that coinhabit the planet with us is to know ourselves better.

We can never experience the world exactly as animals do, but we will use games to help us grow in understanding.

GAME 1: BLIND MAN'S BLUFF

Animal senses are not like our senses. Their perception of the world is different from ours. In this game, a child chosen as IT is blindfolded. Masks, with the eye slots covered with heavy tape, make excellent blindfolds. The child is spun around to disorient him or her. As IT is spinning, the other players run to distant locations and freeze. IT must locate the other players without the use of sight. Other players call out or make sounds, and IT tries to locate the other players by their voices and movements. When IT reaches a player, the sense of touch is used for identification.

Questions for IT: How did you feel as you tried to locate others by sound? Were you able to judge distance?

Ask the class members what they know about bats and eagles? Bats can navigate in total darkness. What other animals can navigate largely by sounds? Radar was based on the hearing of bats; cameras, on the eye of an eagle. Yet even the best of machines cannot approximate the sensitivity and range of animal senses.

GAME 2: MARCO POLO

If you have access to a swimming pool, play Marco Polo. This is another game played without sight, but this time the other players move about in the water in the confines of the pool. IT keeps eyes closed, or wears the mask suggested above. As soon as IT shouts, "Marco," all the other players must answer, "Polo." The object of the game is for IT to catch one of the other players who then becomes "IT." During the game the players keep moving—swimming and running through the water.

This is navigating by sound. Whales and dolphins navigate and communicate by sound phenomenally. Whales send messages to one another over hundreds of miles. Ask class members what other facts they know about whales and dolphins? Think of how we imitate water animals when swimming—for example, the duck-foot flippers of skin divers.

The human view of the world is only one of many. It enriches our understanding of ourselves and our God to move away from familiar worlds and attempt to understand the experience of other animals. Respect for other forms of life might, in some small way, help us work toward preserving the world we share.

View the world from a different perspective. Get down on your hands and knees, like many animals. Crawl around. Look at the world.

Then lie flat on your stomach. Scoot around. Look up and around. What is different about this world?

Now lie on your back. Move in any way you can.

FOR REFLECTION

Leader, you may share with the class if you like.

Playing these games can help teach us that separateness of other creatures is not threatening and so perhaps teach us to live with diversity. Paul Shepherd, in *Thinking Animal*, suggests, "If despite the conflict of deer and wolf . . . or plankton and whale, life survives, then we may also hope to survive our conflicts with the strangers who crowd the human world"—an appropriate message for the world we live in today.

Of course, imagination can go only so far. We can't fully imagine an animal's existence, or a tree's, or what it might be like to open one's flowers on a spring morning. But imagination can give a tiny glimpse of the magnitude and greatness of God's created world.

AND GOD SAID, "IT IS GOOD."

5. Animal Observations

Focusing Scripture

> *And God said, "Let the earth bring forth living creatures of every kind: cattle and creeping things and wild animals of the earth of every kind."*
>
> (GENESIS 1:24)

To Think About

Sensitivity to animals who share our world with us is important. Try for direct experiences in the woods, along the seacoast, in desert regions. Be alert to other creatures that share our world.

Urban children can visit zoos, aquariums, outdoor nature centers, and pet shops.

To reinforce these direct experiences, try these art projects which emphasize the sense of touch as ways of knowing.

Activity

SLIPPERY FROG

Supplies: colored pencils; slender-tipped brush; hide glue (found at hardware stores); a picture of the frog for each student
Step 1: Use colored pencils to color frog.
Step 2: With a slender-tipped brush, "paint" the hide glue over the colored frog.
Hints: Try not to work when the weather is too humid, or the glue will be slow to dry and may feel "tacky." When dry, frog's "skin" should feel slippery.

TEXTURED ELEPHANT

Supplies: 2 copies of the elephant picture for each student; gray water-color paint; white glue; cheesecloth
Step 1: Cut one layer of cheesecloth larger than the actual picture.
Step 2: Spread a thin coat of white glue over the picture, spread the cheesecloth over it, and let dry.
Step 3: Paint the elephant with gray water-color paint, using light, dabbing strokes.

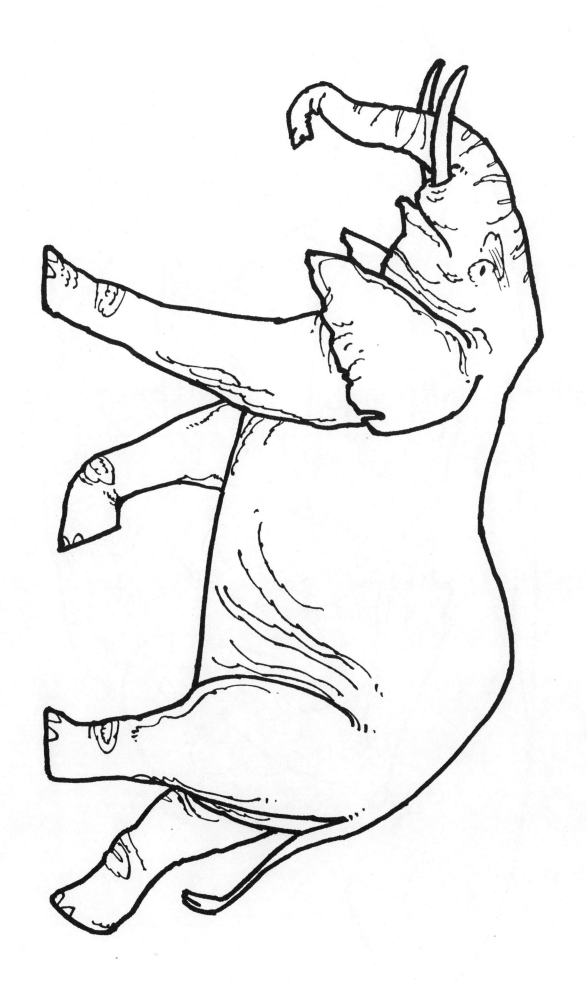

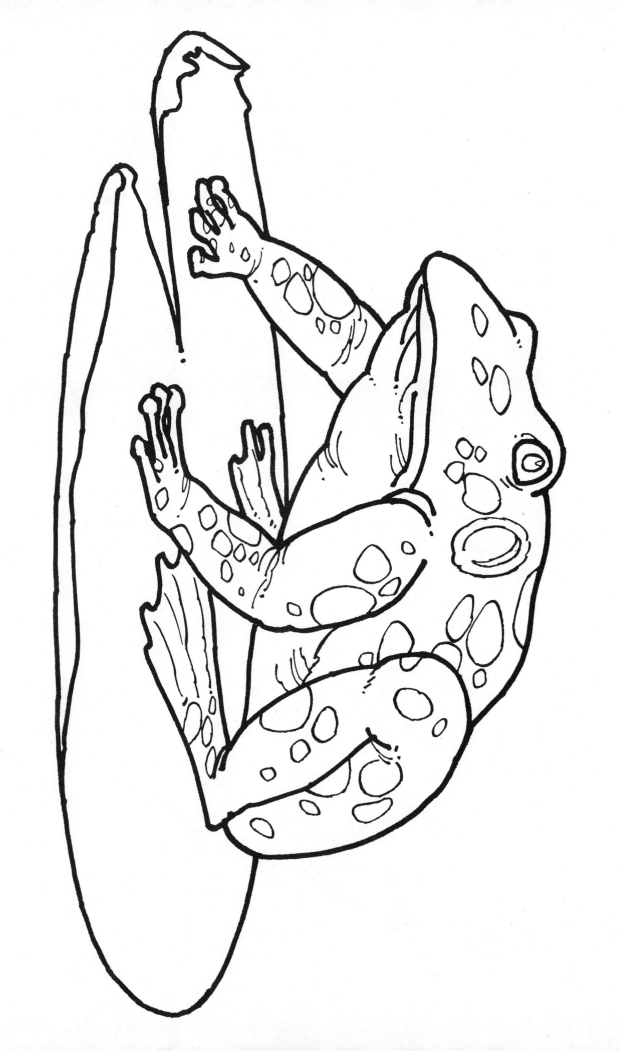

Step 4: When the entire project is dry, cut out the elephant design and glue it on top of the elephant on the second sheet. When complete, the elephant should have skin which appears to be rough and wrinkled, much like that of a real elephant.

As the class members are working on these projects, discuss with them what they should do if a bird or animal is found in the yard. Before picking it up, you should ask yourself the following questions:

1. Does it pose a health hazard to humans or domestic animals?

2. Is it young? Should I leave it where it is, or put it in a safe place nearby?

3. Is it injured? Can I do anything for it, or is it a hopeless case?

4. If I take it home, can I do anything that will enable it to survive and recover enough to be released? If not, am I prepared to look after it as long as it lives?

AND GOD SAID, "IT IS GOOD."

6. Animal Messages

Focusing Scripture

> *The righteous know the needs of their animals,*
> *but the mercy of the wicked is cruel.*
>
> (PROVERBS 12:10)

To Think About

It is interesting to consider the way Native Americans once thought of and lived with our environment. Many still follow this way today. They had great respect for animals. Some believed you should always leave an offering of sage for thanks when you take another living thing for food. This was to thank their spirit for giving up their physical bodies so that the human could live. They killed only for food, never taking more than they needed.

If a hunter from the Seneca nation came upon an animal, he followed the ancient hunter's law of warning his prey by breaking a twig before shooting.

Long ago, a Seneca boy would go alone to the forest or mountain to fast and pray until, in his dreams, an animal, a bird, or some other living creature would appear. This creature would become his protector and helper for the rest of his life.

We have a Bible story in which God used a bird to show the world God's protection and love for Jesus:

Now when all the people were baptized, and when Jesus also had been baptized and was praying, the heaven was opened, and the Holy Spirit descended upon him in bodily form like a dove. And a voice came from heaven, "You are my Son, the Beloved; with you I am well pleased." (Luke 3:21)

Activity

Sit quietly. Reflect on this story about Jesus. Try to bring it vividly to your mind. Imagine the water . . . the sky . . . the dove descending. Now try to imagine how Jesus must have felt—deeply loved and extremely joyful. Jesus probably recalled this event many times during his life, drawing strength and power from the memory.

Let your mind recall a time when you felt deeply loved. Try to really live that experience again. Have you ever given love to and received deep love from a pet? Stay with that feeling, that memory. Reflect on the way we often love our pets just for what they are. Does God love us like this?

Can you remember a time when you felt happy and joyful with an animal? Welcome that joy again to your life. Stay with that scene as long as you experience something of the joy that was yours when the event took place.

Thank God silently for the love and joy that come into our lives through animals—the other living creatures with which we share our world. Poet Samuel Taylor Coleridge captured this idea:

> He prayeth best who loveth best
> All things both great and small;
> For the dear God who loveth us,
> He made and loveth all.
> *(from "The Rime of the Ancient Mariner,"*
> *part VII)*

AND GOD SAID, "IT IS GOOD."

7. Camouflage

Focusing Scripture

> *For I know I am not what I am thought to be.*
> (JOB 9:35)

To Think About

Creatures of all kinds conceal themselves. Look in nature for examples of camouflage:

1. Some animals give false information. The viceroy butterfly looks like the bad-tasting monarch butterfly and birds avoid it.

2. Some animals match their environment, like the African lions who blend into the savannah grasses, the crocodiles who resemble logs, the praying mantis that looks like a twig, cottontail rabbits that freeze into stillness, a white polar bear on a white ice cap.

3. Some animals change colors to camouflage themselves. The chameleon is perhaps the most famous, changing colors within minutes to match its environment. The anole lizard also does this.

4. Some animals change their coloring with the change of seasons. For example, the snowshoe hare becomes white in winter, as do weasels in the north.

Early Christians also had to conceal themselves for protection. Think about this: How would you hide if you were in danger? Where would you hide? How would you communicate with other Christians?

Activity

Here is an example of camouflage writing in a familiar fairy tale. This is the beginning of "Little Red Riding Hood." See if you can figure it out:

LADLE RAT ROTTEN HUT

Wants pawn time, dare worsted ladle gull hoe lift wetter murder inner ladle cordage honor itch offer lodge, dock florist. Disk ladle gull orphan worry ladle cluck wetter putty ladle rat hut, and fur disk raisin pimple colder Ladle Rat Rotten Hut.

Translation: Once upon a time there was a little girl who lived with her mother in a little cottage on the edge of a large, dark forest. This little girl often wore a little cloak with a pretty little red hat and for this reason people called her Little Red Riding Hood.

Using the form of Ladle Rat Rotten Hut, imagine that you were an early follower of the Risen Christ. You were in the upper room and experienced the coming of the Holy Spirit at Pentecost (Acts 2). You want to share this experience with your friends and neighbors, but are afraid of being discovered. Write this experience in code.

AND GOD SAID, "IT IS GOOD."

8. Flowing Streams

Focusing Scripture

On the last day of the festival, the great day, while Jesus was standing there, he cried out, "Let anyone who is thirsty come to me, and let the one who believes in me drink. As the scripture has said, 'Out of the believer's heart shall flow rivers of living water.'"

(JOHN 7:37-38)

To Think About

Among the most refreshing joys of nature is a running stream of water (a creek or current of water flowing in a definite direction). Children describe the sound of a creek as "happy" and "skipping."

Activity

Go on a hike with your class, following a stream or creek. Listen to the song of the water. As you follow it, notice how the pitch and sound change as the water goes around rocks or jumps to a different level.

Notice colors. Deep streams are dark, while shallow ones are bright and sparkling. Allow all your senses to enjoy this experience. Sniff the thin, spray-cooled air. Watch the stream's journey. See how it shatters to foam as it passes over sunken rocks. Watch as it races ahead. Listen to the hiss and splash and gurgle, the whisper of blown and scattered spray. A stream is full of surprises as it meanders in and out of rocky outcrops . . . runs wide and lazy in spots . . . creates waterfalls.

It can be entertaining just to sit and watch the movement, the sparkling spray changing color in the sunlight, the unexpected things that float by.

It's fun to float things in a moving stream—pieces of bark, branches, seed pods, nuts, leaves. Enjoy this pleasure with your class. Find a shallow, moving place in the stream where the class members can wade and race their "boats." Have a floating race. Start at a common point and have spotters stand at the finish line to see which crosses first. Afterward, reflect on this experience:

1. Think about how this stream is affecting the ground around it. Little by little, year after year, the water is cutting away the ground. A fast-moving stream carries not only water but fine particles,

pebbles, gravel, and boulders along with it. Some think the Grand Canyon, with its great size, was created by the year-after-year flow of the river.

Think about your life. All the church services and Sunday school classes you attend are forming your life. They may not seem to be powerful forces, but little-by-little, they are creating the person you are and are going to be.

2. Think about how your life moves along like an object in a stream. Perhaps your little boat ran into "eddies" (little currents that move against the general flow, creating small whirlpools). Could your boat float around the obstacle, or did it get caught and pulled in? Were there times when your boat slowed down and had to be given a gentle push? How can this experience speak to your spiritual life?

3. A symbol for the church is a boat. Think of all the ways you can to compare the journey of your boat and the journey of your church.

4. Think about how few streams follow straight courses. A stream with looping curves is said to meander. Where does your stream meander? How might this speak to your life or the life of your church?

5. Play with sponges in the water—slurp and sloosh the water up into the sponge. Reflect with the class members on the fact that they live in God the way sponges live in water. May you always be as open to God as a sponge is open to water.

Additional Activities

If it is impossible to visit a stream, play with a hose. Imagine that the water is a great stream of love and peace. Aim it at people you love. Aim it at people you don't love. Finally, let it flow abundantly, indiscriminately, to animals, birds, trees. Water the flowers. Spray in such a way as to make a rainbow.

Make a Water Picture: Sprinkle dry tempera paint on butcher paper. Then lightly spray the picture with water and watch the colors run to create a new picture. Or you could put your paper outdoors when the rain is falling lightly.

AND GOD SAID, "IT IS GOOD."

9. Deep Pools of Water

Focusing Scripture

> *He leads me beside still waters;*
> *he restores my soul.*
> (PSALM 23:2b-3a)

To Think About

The feeling of a deep pool of water is different from that of a running stream. There is peace and mystery when one looks into the dark or reflecting depths.

Find a deep pool of water, a pond, or a lake. If this is impossible, meditate on a picture of still water. Share the following with your class:

Water has always been a powerful symbol of our faith. Whatever our tradition, baptism is a cleansing act. Going down into the water is symbolic of dying with Christ; coming up, rising with Christ. Baptism declares that we are received by God only on the basis of what Christ has done for us. Then we are not just received, but incorporated into Christ.

Read the Bible story of the healing in the pool at Bethseda (John 5:1-9). Reflect on Jesus' question: "Do you want to be healed?"

Activity

1. Learn the song "You Called Me."

You Called Me

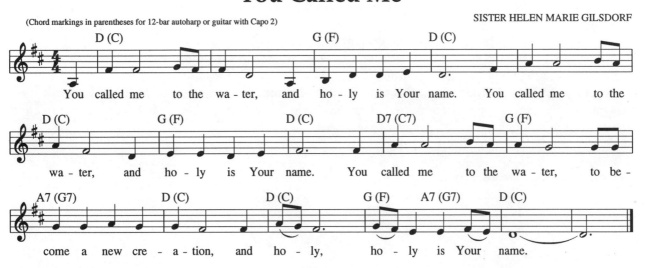

SISTER HELEN MARIE GILSDORF

Used with permission of Resource Publications, Inc., Copyright © 1978, 160 E. Virginia St. #290, San Jose, CA 95112

2. Put a small packet of salt in your mouth. Fast-food stores are generous with these and each packet contains just the right amount. Let the taste remain in your mouth as the music plays softly. An alternative is to use oyster crackers. Both produce a feeling of dryness and thirst symbolic of a soul thirsting for God.

3. As the class is experiencing the salt, say Psalm 143:6b: "My soul thirsts for you like a parched land."

4. Then invite the class to enjoy the refreshment of a cool drink of water. As your taste buds are restored, so your soul is restored by the presence of God. Let the water move you into a deeper serenity and mindfulness. Become aware of your own inner calm, like that of a deep pool of water.

Activity

Another way to experience this in the classroom is to let a plant dry out. Watch the leaves droop and wither. Then water it and see how quickly it responds.

AND GOD SAID, "IT IS GOOD."

10. Mud

Focusing Scripture

> *[God] will come to us like the showers,*
> *like the spring rains that water the earth.*
>
> (HOSEA 6:3*b*)

Activity

It's great fun to take a rain hike with your class—a walk out of the ordinary. Bundled up in rain garb, go out into the rain. Smell the damp earth. Feel the soft drops on your face. Look at the richness of colors. Discover how leaves funnel off the water. Try to spot animals and notice how they shelter themselves. See how a place with which you are familiar seems to change during a rain.

Especially during the spring thaw, enjoy mud . . . mud . . . glorious mud. Take off your shoes and feel it squish between your toes. Pat it into mud cakes.

Afterward, clean up and act out this wonderful mud story from Judges 4:4-14 in the Bible. *Experiment with the class to find a metal sound that represents the sound of 900 chariots. Try hitting jangling keys or tapping metal objects with a pencil. Be creative.*

DEBORAH'S VICTORY

Three characters: Deborah: a wise judge
Barak: a fearful general
Narrator

Scene 1

(Class makes metal sound, directed by teacher.)

Barak: What's that? What is that sound?

Deb: It's the 900 iron chariots of Sisera. They are roaming our countryside again.

Barak: *(trembling)* They are looking for people to capture and carry away. Oh woe! Woe! You don't know what it is like. I was captured when I was young and taken into the household of Sisera himself. Oh it was terrible—terrible! Now I'm so afraid. I slink along back roads and hide in caves.

Deb: I'm ashamed of you, Barak—you, a general. We are the children of the one true God. These people of Canaan worship false gods. God has told me that we will defeat these Canaanites, and I will now name the warrior who is going to lead us into victorious battle. It is you—Barak!

Barak: What?

Deb: Yes! You are the general. You will battle and defeat Sisera and his 900 chariots.

Barak: *(stuttering)* Hhhhhhow can we wwwwin against Ssssisera? We have no cccchariots.

Deb: We have something far better. We have God on our side.

Barak: Oh all right—but I have one request. *(Falls on his knees and grabs Deborah around her knees.)* Please go with me.

Deb: I'll go with you, Barak. My goodness, you are a sissy.

Narrator: Will Barak ever be able to lead warriors into battle? Can he win against 900 chariots? Is Deborah right? We'll soon see.

Scene 2

Deb: Well, here we are, Barak, on top of Mount Tabor. The wonderful moment of victory is not far away. Soon Sisera and all his men will be coming after us.

Barak: That's what I'm afraid of.

Deb: Listen—I think I hear them coming.
(Class makes metal sound again.)
Yes—Yes. There they are. What an impressive sight they are—circling in their chariots down in the valley.

Barak: Oh, we're all going to be killed. I know it. What's that? I feel something. It's rain. Not only do we fight against impossible odds—now we have to fight in the rain. Oh woe! Woe!

Deb: God's help has come.

Barak: The rain is pouring. The creek is overflowing. We are all doomed!

Deb: Look! Sisera's chariots are getting stuck in the mud. They can't maneuver at all. Now look—the soldiers are running away! We are winning! Barak, you are a great general. The iron chariots are gone for good, and so is Sisera!

Barak: We won? I won?

Deb: Congratulations!

Barak: I won't ever have to be afraid again? Whoopee!

Deb: God made the rainstorm, the mud, and the clay. All our enemies are scattered away.

AND GOD SAID, "IT IS GOOD!"

AFTERNOON

Behold!

You are indeed my rock and my fortress;
for your name's sake lead me and guide me.
(PSALM 31:3)

Ask the animals, and they will teach you;
the birds of the air, and they will tell you.
(JOB 12:7)

Out of the believer's heart
shall flow rivers of living water.
(JOHN 7:38*b*)

And God said, "Let the earth bring forth living creatures of every kind: cattle and creeping things."
(GENESIS 1:24)

He leads me beside still waters;
he restores my soul.
(PSALM 23:2a-3*b*)

[God] will come to us like the showers,
like the spring rains that water the earth.
(HOSEA 6:3*b*)

Chapter Five

TWILIGHT

Entering the Mystery

Twilight, the closing of the day, is a time of ingathering not unlike the season of autumn. The dark time is approaching. Again we pause to reflect on new discoveries made in the afternoon and to prepare ourselves for the coming darkness. We linger for a moment at this time between.

We gather in the fruits of this day and ponder them. How can we help giving thanks? We rejoice in the goodness of the earth and of human life. So much has been given us this day.

We notice how nature raises a flame against the darkness with aspen glows and radiant sunsets, brilliant leaves and fall wildflowers, and we affirm that the mystery of God's love is stronger than darkness. Four of the activities in this section celebrate this radiance.

Relating to nature at twilight seems a more gentle activity. *Tender* seems to describe the feeling of twilight. As the day retreats, in nature there is caring rather than controlling, harmony rather than mastery. Twilight seems characterized by humility rather than arrogance, by appreciation rather than acquisitiveness. Like an ache, we are aware of the beauty, the goodness and the vulnerability that exists everywhere.

We sit around a twilight campfire and hear again our Bible stories. We let the words wash over us. These familiar stories relate us to a larger mystery. The smoke and firelight glow remind us of this mystery residing at the center of creation. We realize the awe-filled, yet most comfortable truth that our Creator God is all wise, all loving, all great—this Holy Mystery who is named God, yet is ultimately unnameable.

And then with eyes of faith, we can join the writer of Genesis, enter the mystery and see "the LORD God walking in the garden in the cool of the day" (3:8 KJV).

1. Autumn Walk

Focusing Scripture

> The LORD your God, who is present with you, is a great and awesome God.
>
> (DEUTERONOMY 7:21)

To Think About

An autumn walk is a feast for all the senses, a direct communication to the emotions, bringing a sense of affirmation and wonder.

Wildflowers have changed their look—purple asters and goldenrod dance, foreshadowing the last blooms of the year. Many plants sport berries now, rather than blossoms. Seeds and seed pods abound in interesting and sometimes grotesque shapes. Notice the milkweed pods and cattails and tall beautiful grasses. Leaves crunch underfoot as you walk. Perhaps you hear the call of migrating birds or see woodland animals beginning to thicken their coats.

The air has a different scent—of straw and husks and fall herbs. The produce of autumn spills over as if from a horn of plenty—crisp apples and fat orange pumpkins, golden wheat and corn. Nuts that plop to the ground are collected by scampering squirrels. There may be the glistening of first frost. You can know autumn in your eyes and ears and nostrils, on your tongue, and in your entire being.

Activity

Bring magazines with pictures of autumn into your classroom. Let the class members flip through these magazines at random, pausing when a picture of autumn splendor particularly grips them. Have the students cut or tear out these pictures. When each student has one or more, stop and let them share their particular prized autumn images. You are creating an atmosphere of appreciation. You want to capture the look, the smell, the taste, the feel, the whole sense of life in autumn—the marvel of it—the glory. We rejoice in the goodness of the earth.

With eyes instructed by these images, send the students out into a nature area to gather and bring back some small item that symbolizes or could help illustrate their faith journey. Suggest leaves, pods, bark, cones. When all are assembled again, the students share and explains their objects.

Then invite the students to press the nature material that represents their faith symbols into stoneware clay. Then remove to make impressions and let the clay dry. It may be left as is or baked according to package directions.

Say: Let this object become a talisman for you to carry with you or place where you can see it. This talisman, or symbol, means that God spoke to you through this nature object. It communicates what words cannot, and at a different level. We draw near to God when we are close to the things God has made.

Conclude with an autumn treat. Eat popcorn, puffed wheat, a wheat/rice cold cereal mixture. Drink apple cider.

AND GOD SAID, "IT IS GOOD."

2. Leaf Radiance

Focusing Scripture

> *The glory of the LORD appeared to them.*
> (NUMBERS 20:6b)

To Think About

Just after the frosting of the summer flowers and before they are buried in snow, there comes a festival season when nature is all aglow—a blast of color. Sometime in early October or late September, the leaves in the northern part of the United States begin to turn radiant colors—brilliant red, fiery orange, shimmering gold, rich purple. Sunlight glistens and glows through these autumn leaves. Help your students become aware of this spectacle.

Science tells us that the brilliant colors of autumn leaves are actually present all year, but the colors are masked by the chlorophyll which our eyes perceive as green. Once the chlorophyll begins to break down, the underlying colors show through. Perhaps in the same way, we are missing images of God, always present in nature but masked for us in some way.

Activity

Some time in the fall, take your class out on a walk to collect leaves.

Back in the classroom, read Matthew 4:23-5:1, 8:1, and 9:35-36. Invite the class members to use their imaginations to envision the crowds that followed Jesus.

With these pictures in their minds, give each student a large sheet of art paper on which to place the collected leaves. Now let the shapes of the various leaves suggest people. Move them around on the paper to create a scene of Jesus and the crowds. Try the leaves upside down or sideways until a person's image appears to you. Is there a special leaf that suggests Jesus? Where will you place it? Are there Pharisees with long flowing robes? Do Linden leaves suggest plump tax collectors? Are mountain ash leaves like little children clinging to their mothers? Do maple leaves seem like persons reaching out to be healed or touched? Are partial or nibbled leaves suggesting the wounded? Do the leaves bring to mind remembered Bible stories?

When you are satisfied with your scenes, trace around the leaves on the paper. Then remove each leaf and add features to the imagined people.

Share your pictures and study all of them for insight and understanding. Autumn leaves can remind us that all of creation is a sacramental presence, pointing to something more. Carry with you through the day these words: "When he saw the crowds, he had compassion for them, because they were harassed and helpless" (Matt. 9:36).

AND GOD SAID, "IT IS GOOD."

3. The Aspen Glow

Focusing Scripture

God . . . has shone in our hearts to give the light of the knowledge of the glory of God in the face of Jesus Christ.

(II CORINTHIANS 4:6*b*)

To Think About

Have you seen it—the radiant shining? Once I saw a radiance, the aspen glow. Enchanted by the beauty of the giant trees in the Mariposa Grove at Yosemite National Park, my husband and I gazed too long—going farther and farther up the mountain, mesmerized by the overpowering size of those trees. We hiked up and up. We looked too long upon the fallen remains of one of these giants, walking round and round it.

Suddenly we realized we were alone. The other tourists and hikers had been gone for some time. Darkness was falling quickly, and we were miles from our car. We hurried, in a stumbling run, past tree giants that were assuming menacing shapes, past glints of animal eyes appearing in the semidarkness.

Then near the bottom of the mountain, looking back, we saw the flush of the aspen glow. Who can describe it? The mountains, holding the last light of the sun, gleamed with an unearthly radiance. They were transformed into polished jewels, reflecting and giving off their own light—apricot-colored, iridescent—unlike anything I had ever seen or experienced. Above the gigantic shadows of the monstrous black shapes of trees, it glowed and glowed—radiance that was shining . . . shining . . . shining.

Activity

PLAY A GAME

Divide the class into two teams. Give each team two minutes to list all the things they can think of in nature that glow—that have their own iridescent light.

OR

HAVE A QUIET TIME

- Think back on the day. Reflect quietly about the different lights of nature.
- Think of the different shades of light you have seen this day.
- Have you ever heard the phrase "seeing yourself in a different light"? How might you use this phrase as you think about yourself and God?
- Jesus said, "You are the light of the world." There is light within you. Reach deep and let it out.
- Have you ever seen a glow of happiness on someone's face? Hum, or sing as a round, "Dona Nobis Pacem."

AND GOD SAID, "IT IS GOOD."

4. Sunset

Focusing Scripture

The sun knows its time for setting.

(PSALM 104:19*b*)

To Think About

Each day, a spectacular new picture is painted, framed, and held up for half an hour—the sunset—a nature gift that belongs to everyone. Yet how many times do we stop and notice it? We realize, with a start, that the sunset is there to be found if we look for it, though not demanding our attention.

The great arch of the sky reminds us that our God is a dying and rising God. Jesus came to earth to show us this aspect of God, which has always been there—a dying and rising God. Each day the sunset reminds us of this great truth, this great mystery.

As we view a sunset in the sweep of sky, we begin with seeing it as "pretty." As we continue to watch, we move through successive stages to "beautiful." The changing sequence of colors enchants us, becoming potent, efficacious, and therapeutic. We are enveloped in the huge wash of colors. Warm colors excite, cool colors tranquilize, bright colors stimulate, dark tones relax, and the sequence, rather than the sameness, moves us beyond the beautiful to values as yet uncaptured by language. We absorb this beauty and knowledge rather than logically learn it. We forget the scientific explanations—that dust and pollen and floating particles cause this spectacle—and simply, as a poet once said, "Enjoy what others understand."

Activity

In the presence of a sunset, read the story of the Transfiguration in Mark 9:2-8 or Luke 9:28-36. This is perhaps the most powerful image we have of a totally transformed human being. Like a sunset, there was a sequence of color.

Look for the dazzling gold of the setting sun. If you are in a location where this is reflected off a body of water, you will see it resplendent and sparkling. Imagine this shining magnificence reflected in Jesus' face and appearance.

Watch the parade of clouds in the sunset. Pick out "dazzling white" (Mark 9:3).

Observe the reaches of the clouds sending down ribbons of color. Imagine the most beautiful as the one from which God spoke (Luke 9:34).

Watch the changing colors and the vastness. Reflect on the story. How could this happen? It doesn't matter how. Time and deliberation are required for adequate appreciation. That's the way the whole Bible is—stories concealing much deeper levels, colorful narration wrapped around the essence of mystery—broad and deep in meaning and mystery, and difficult to fully understand.

Continue to watch and ponder. As the sun sets, there is a sense of stillness like that which follows a pageant that has just gone by. Who can see where it goes? The incredible beauty can never be fully grasped. Nature converts itself into a vast promise. There is more—much more.

AND GOD SAID, "IT IS GOOD!"

5. Voices Crying in the Wilderness

Focusing Scripture

> *The voice of one crying out in the wilderness.*
> (MATTHEW 3:3b)

To Think About

A twilight campfire is the perfect setting for the following stories and experiences. The rising smoke affirms the mystery and incorporeality of God. Gazing into the fire, we remember the presence of the sacred in our midst. Invite the children to be quiet so that they can hear God's word of warmth and care in the fire. Toss in some cedar boughs to add aroma. Fire is a magic, mysterious medium, which speaks of the power of God and nature.

As we sit around a campfire in a wilderness area, it is interesting to remember that a wilderness experience is very much a part of our religious heritage. Both Jesus and Moses sojourned in the wilderness to prepare for their holy missions.

A biblical character also often associated with the wilderness is John the Baptist. Read his story in all four of the Gospels: Matthew 3; Mark 1:2-11; Luke 3:1-23; John 1:15-34.

Can you imagine John, clothed in a rough garment of camel's hair with a belt of skin, stepping out of the twilight shadows to speak to you? Stepping out from the wilderness—a messenger from God?

John, a cousin of Jesus, had grown up alone in desert country, listening to God's voice. He did not go to the city to preach but stayed in the wilderness of Judea near the River Jordan. He ate the simple food he found in the wilderness—dried locusts and wild honey. In describing himself, John said, "I am the voice of one crying out in the wilderness, 'Make straight the way of the Lord'" (John 1:23).

Activity

Listen to the wilderness sounds around you. Listen for the twilight sounds of one crying in the wilderness. Can you hear a moan in the wind?—a sigh or cry in the fire? Sometimes the twilight wind says, "Yes . . . yes . . . yes." Sometimes the wind will rise to a howl eerily human in timbre—chilling to hear.

Perhaps you will hear animal sounds—the lonesome howl of a dog, or even a wolf or coyote. Whippoorwills repeat their plaintive song. Sit quietly and listen. Say to yourself, "The voice of one crying out in the wilderness." The sounds might remind you of some experience you need to mourn or grieve over.

Insect sounds may be heard—those of crickets and katydids are thermometers. They chirp fast when the weather is warm, slower and slower as it gets colder. When they are silent—fall is here.

One very strange sound you may hear in the twilight has been called the devil's fiddle. It is created when one tree has fallen and been caught by a branch of another tree. As evening winds blow and move the branches against each other, an unearthly sound is created—strange and haunting, unlike anything you may have heard before—perhaps a voice crying in the wilderness.

An interesting velvety sound is heard at twilight as birds, often in flocks, pass through the air. It is rare music, with calls and chirps and some song notes—full of reality, full of illusion.

Tune your ears for cries in the wilderness. Be alert to these wonderful sounds. Let the sounds remind you of our Bible stories of John the Baptist: "Look out! Prepare! Be Ready!" Remember this story of our faith and find yourself in the story.

Meditate on Romans 8:26. We do not know how to pray as we ought, but that very Spirit intercedes with sighs too deep for words.

Then recall the beautiful promise included in John the Baptist's message in Luke 3:5a, 6a, as he quoted the prophet Isaiah: "Every valley shall be filled, and every mountain and hill shall be made low . . . and all flesh shall see the salvation of God."

AND GOD SAID, "IT IS GOOD."

6. Strange and Wonderful Things

Focusing Scripture

> *And even this was a small thing in your sight, O God.*
> (I CHRONICLES 17:17)

To Think About

Around a twilight campfire, we hear the story of Peter walking on the water—a strange and mysterious event.

After nightfall, a strong wind began to blow across the sea. Rowing as hard as they might, the disciples could not make much progress against the wind. Higher and higher the waves dashed and rolled. Slower and slower the vessel plowed through them. The disciples were very tired. They wished for Jesus' presence.

Jesus knew how much they needed him, and he started to them, out across the water. He walked as easily as if he had been on land. How could he do this? The disciples did not believe what they were seeing. No person had ever done that. But Jesus did, and he came to them.

This is a strange story. The Bible is full of strange happenings. Moses parts the Red Sea, and the children of Israel walk across. Joshua blows a trumpet, and walls come tumbling down. You can think of other stories of happenings that were wonderful and awesome. "[He] does great things beyond understanding, and marvelous things without number" (Job 9:10). God's creation is full of strange, unexplainable things.

Vivian Brown, in *Investigating Nature Through Outdoor Projects,* tells of viewing a full-moon rabbit dance. In a fairly open wood near a thicket of blackberries, she saw rabbits form several circles and jump and dance. As she watched, the rabbits jumped higher and higher. There was mad twirling and a frenzy of excitement. She described it as "a rare and wonderful sight—a thrilling look into the life of the night."

Many naturalists write of seeing a green flash at sunset—momentary but extraordinary, completely unexpected but recorded too many times to be untrue.

There are records throughout history of a phenomenon in nature called Saint Elmo's fire. It is described as a bluish or greenish flame-shaped light, accompanied by a sizzling or crackling noise, usually seen on the tops of trees or high steeples during stormy or threatening weather.

The Aurora Borealis is a brilliant luminous phenomenon in the northern hemisphere, with a variety of colors and shapes. It is radiant energy emitted from definite regions in the upper atmosphere.

The Great Barrier Reef, along the northern coast of Australia, reveals extraordinary beauties of shifting light and color.

A banyan tree grows from a thousand trunks.

The deserts, the caves, the volcanoes, the noise and mist of Niagara Falls—these are wonders so enormous they seem unreal.

Activity

Ask your students, using a whispering voice of awe, what amazing things they have seen or experienced through nature.

Invite your students to close their eyes and think about what someone once observed: "If you have never heard the mountains singing or seen the trees of the field clapping their hands, do not think because of that they don't. Ask God to open your ears so you may hear it and your eyes so you may see it, because though few men ever know it, they do, my friends, they do."

Say: We want to stretch our minds now. Think about all these things and let the wonder deepen.

Nature makes the mind boggle and gasp in astonishment. It is the same with Christianity. Faith is the breakthrough into that deep realm of the soul which accepts paradox and mystery with humility.

Augustine said, "If you understand it, it isn't God." Think about what that means.

AND GOD SAID, "IT IS GOOD."

7. Watchers at the Crucifixion

Focusing Scripture

Many women were also there, looking on from a distance; they had followed Jesus from Galilee and had provided for him. Among them were Mary Magdalene, and Mary the mother of James and Joseph, and the mother of the sons of Zebedee.

(MATTHEW 27:55-56)

And when all the crowds who had gathered there for this spectacle saw what had taken place, they returned home, beating their breasts. But all his acquaintances, including the women who had followed him from Galilee, stood at a distance, watching these things.

(LUKE 23:48-49)

84

To Think About

Twilight is a time to read these Bible verses with appreciation. The approaching darkness, the half-light, the partial shadows, cause us to look and "almost see." Approaching shadows, perhaps accompanied by rising mists, call us—an invitation to a mystery. Magical, changing images are born of these shadows; veiled illusions are seen.

Sit, looking at a landscape. (One with woods and rocks is especially appropriate.) Find pictures and shapes in the shadows. What do the trees look like? Bring into focus images from the shadows and the bare branches of trees in silhouette. Can you imagine those persons at the crucifixion—watching from a distance?

Observe gray, the marvelous neutral color in nature. It is especially interesting at twilight. Try to distinguish tones of gray around you. Can you find in nature these delineations of gray: steel gray, iron gray, dove gray, slate gray, silver gray, other tones of gray?

Gray has been described as the intermediate color between heaven and earth. Ponder this description. Look at the rocks that have lain under the heavens so long. Can you imagine them as solidified air, with a tinge of earth? Think about this definition as your mind tries to understand "incarnation." It is hard for our minds to grasp the idea that Jesus was both "God" and "man." Let the image of the rock help you understand: earth and sky—God and man. If it doesn't make sense to the logical mind, we can "know" and understand at a deeper level.

Think about how gray makes the most discordant materials harmonize—the color of unpainted wood, weather-stained and time-stained—hard, enduring gray.

Watch gray shadows appearing on the landscape. Place a cross in the ground at a location where the setting sun will cause it to form a shadow. Watch the shadow grow as the sun sets. Look at the pattern. Remember our Bible stories of the crucifixion. Let the two images merge in your mind. Notice how the shadow slowly moves forward. Draw wisdom and understanding from this observation.

Add the dimension of music by humming, "Were You There When They Crucified My Lord?"

Activity

Sketch with charcoal these twilight images you have seen. Smudge shadows on the paper with your fingers.

AND GOD SAID, "IT IS GOOD."

8. Music in Nature

Focusing Scripture

On that day David first appointed the singing of praises to the LORD. . . . Then all the people said "Amen" and praised the LORD.

(I CHRONICLES 16:7, 36c)

To Think About

There is beautiful music in nature for those with ears to hear. Thoreau, a great lover of nature, said, "Ah, if I could put into words the music which I hear."

There are the sounds of grand murmurs, underlying vibrations: the surf, the wind in the forest, waterfalls. Essentially, they seem one sound—the earth voice, a natural sound that brings peace and harmony, a murmur through the universe.

To my ears, that earth voice sounds like an "A" and an "M." We can make the sound by letting the tone begin in the throat and vibrate through the nasal cavity until the head and body tingle with the sound. It is as if we tune ourselves like instruments to the symphony of the universe. It is like tuning ourselves to the Spirit of God.

Activity

1. When Moses asked God who he was, God answered, "I AM WHO I AM" (Exod. 3:14).

If your class is receptive to the idea, you can sit in a tight circle, eyes closed, and chant, "I AM." Feel yourself at one with God and the entire universe.

2. Another activity, using the A and M murmur sound of the earth, is to chant the word *amazing* on a pitch (D-G on piano). This continues as an ostinato. After a time, part of the class sings the hymn "Amazing Grace" as the murmur sound of "Amazing" continues underneath.

3. A third use of the A and M murmur sound of the earth is to chant the word *Amen*. Then use the chant as a response in the following prayer:

Leader: The pounding surf upon the shore says:
Class: AMEN

The blowing of a conch shell says: AMEN
The whispering of the winds says: AMEN
The noise of the flowing rivers says: AMEN
The shifting sands in the desert say: AMEN
The rustle of leaves in the forest says: AMEN
The lowing of herds of cattle says: AMEN
The sound of a gong says: AMEN
The lapping of lakes upon the shore says: AMEN
The rotation of stars and planets says: AMEN
The roar of mountains in winter says: AMEN
A multitude of living creatures say: AMEN
The sibilant sighs of pine trees say: AMEN
The gruff grumbles of oak trees say: AMEN
The quaking, trembling aspen says: AMEN
The sizzle sound of falling snow says: AMEN
The silver patter of rain says: AMEN

God is producing sounds all around us, so that when they are registered on our eardrums, we shall hear God and join the great—AMEN!

AND GOD SAID, "IT IS GOOD."

9. Birds That Sing in the Cold

Focusing Scripture

I will sing of your might;
I will sing aloud of your steadfast love in the morning.   (PSALM 59:16)

By the streams the birds of the air have their habitation;
they sing among the branches.   (PSALM 104:12)

To Think About

John Muir, the naturalist, often wrote about his favorite bird—the water ouzel, or water thrush. The size of a robin, blue-gray with a tinge of chocolate on the head and shoulders, the water thrush, according to Muir, is always "joyous and lovable." This bird, infrequently seen, lives near falling water—waterfalls and cascades. It flits through the spraying water and dives into the foaming eddies, ever vigorous and enthusiastic. This thrush will follow waterfalls through their darkest gorges, always singing, pouring its shower of notes into the plunging water. In the most desperately cold and unpleasant weather, Muir felt inspired by the downright gladness of this bird's song.

A friend who lives high on a mountain in North Carolina tells me that on still, dark winter afternoons, she is often startled by the outrageously joyful singing of a little Carolina wren that comes very close to her window. And naturalist Loren Eiseley tells of being inspired by hearing a bird sing happily in the midst of a cold, driving rain. Birds that sing in the cold speak to us of hope and of another way of being in the world.

We pause to ponder: Are humans the only beings in nature that despair? When we feel our lives are not worth much, we must remember that God planned our liberation from despair by sending Jesus to us. Birdsong reminds us.

Ask: Have you ever heard a bird sing in winter? Where were you, and what was the occasion?

It is said that birdsong must be learned anew each generation, the young birds taught by their elders. Can you recall a time in your life when you saw someone who was grateful and glad in the midst of a difficult situation? Share this with the class.

Activity

Sing with the class the chorus of the spiritual, "Every Time I Feel the Spirit." Then the students fill in these words as each writes his or her own lines of this song:

A SONG TO SING IN THE COLD

When I am _____ _____ _____ (three words or syllables)

When I am sad

I will remember _____ _____ _____ (three words or syllables)

And be glad.

Going around the class, the students say their words. Then all join in singing the chorus again.

AND GOD SAID, "IT IS GOOD."

TWILIGHT
Entering the Mystery

The LORD your God, who is present with
you, is a great and awesome God.
(DEUTERONOMY 7:21)

God . . . has shone in our hearts
to give the light of the knowledge of
the glory of God in the face of Jesus Christ.
(II CORINTHIANS 4:6b)

And even this was a small thing in your
sight, O God.
(I CHRONICLES 17:17)

By the streams the birds of the air
have their habitation;
they sing among the branches.
(PSALM 104:12)

The voice of one crying out in the
wilderness.
(MATTHEW 3:3b)

The sun knows its time for setting.
(PSALM 104:19b)

Chapter Six

EVENING

Letting Go

-- -- -- -- -- -- -- -- -- -- -- -- -- -- -- -- --

In the west, the sun sinks. The world loses its light. Flowers enfold themselves. Birds cease their singing. People yield to sleep. The exquisite uncertainty of twilight is replaced with a knowing, an acceptance of peace. The temperature turns warmer or cooler by a degree or two. Instead of flowers underfoot, there are stars overhead. The time has come for us to stop—from the discoveries and the learning and the wondering, the pondering and the adventurings. We stop and let it all go.

But night also brings fears of a dark, cold nature. The life-giving power of the sun is gone. The activities of the day are over. Anxieties surface.

When our son was very small, he had an interesting reaction to the dark. Entering a dark room, he would begin to call himself: "Neel? Neel?" His voice would become more and more anxious until a light was turned on. It was as if he had lost himself in the dark. Perhaps that feeling is not too far from all of us.

In our spiritual life, as in the evening, a moment comes when we let go and come face to face with our true selves. We release our angers and worries and fears. We surrender to God in complete trust, as a small child lies down to sleep. We rest and gather strength for another day.

In this evening section, four of the activities emphasize letting go of things that separate us from God—worries and fears and anger and busyness.

This section also includes some uniquely evening activities—a night walk, some bedtime activities, and a look at the final letting go—death.

1. Worries

Focusing Scripture

Do not worry about tomorrow, for tomorrow will bring worries of its own. Today's trouble is enough for today.

(MATTHEW 6:34)

To Think About

The human mind is restless. It looks to future events with fear or anticipation. It looks to the past with nostalgia or guilt. Sometimes we love our anxieties. We cling to them and wallow in them. The Good News of the gospel is that we are not to live that way, and nature helps us to realize this.

The vastness of nature has a way of absorbing our worries and anxieties. Being in a natural setting helps us to put our little lives in perspective. Nature is a place where we can let go of our worries and anxieties.

Activity:

Gather the class in a quiet circle. Read Elizabeth Barrett Browning's poem, "A New Perspective":

> The little cares that fretted me,
> I lost them yesterday
> Among the fields above the sea,
> Among the winds at play;
> Among the lowing of the herds,
> The rustling of the trees,
> Among the singing of the birds,
> The humming of the bees.
> The foolish fears of what may happen,
> I cast them all away
> Among the clover-scented grass,
> Among the new-mown hay;
> Among the husking of the corn
> Where drowsy poppies nod,
> Where ill thoughts die
> and good are born.
> Out in the fields with God.

Invite the class to take a few deep breaths and think about the poem. Think how the solitude of nature is a remedy for our normal worrisome days. We forget the mean, the narrow, the trivial, and focus on the beautiful.

Reflect on the day. Ask: What did you see today that was beautiful? What did you hear that was pleasing? What did you touch that was moving?

If you are sitting around a campfire or an indoor fireplace, hit a log in the fire with the poker. Ask the children to count the sparks that fly. Can they name a blessing from the day for each spark they see?

The leader makes a list of the blessings in categories: sight, sound, touch. Items listed will hold no element of terror.

Quietly and slowly, the leader reads again the words in each category. The children respond to each category by humming or singing the refrain to the hymn, "It Is Well with My Soul."

Then everyone quietly goes off to dreams and visions.

AND GOD SAID, "IT IS GOOD."

2. Fears

Focusing Scripture

> When I am afraid,
> I put my trust in you.
> (PSALM 56:3)

> Do not fear, for I am with you,
> do not be afraid, for I am your God;
> I will strengthen you, I will help you,
> I will uphold you with my victorious right hand.
> (ISAIAH 41:10)

To Think About

Read or tell the story of Jesus' temptations in the wilderness (Matt. 4:1-11; Mark 1:12; Luke 4:1-14).

Many people fear or "hate" some things in nature. Thinking about Jesus alone in the wilderness will encourage your students to suggest fears that they might have in such a situation.

Activity

List things the class fears or hates.

What animals?
- snakes?
- spiders?
- bats?
- wild animals?

What about the unknown?
- fear of the dark?
- fear of being lost?
- fear of thunder?

What about things that injure?
- thorns and stickers?
- quills on porcupines?
- horns and antlers?
- insect bites?

Things that offend the senses?
- skunks?
- poison ivy?

Many times, a discussion of fears make them less intense. When all the fears have been listed, offer a positive for every negative. What animals in nature do you like? What can you know and count on in nature? What are some soft things in nature? What are some pleasant things?

Add the dimension of a symbol. Put the name of each category of fear on a small candle. Let a child who is fearful light the candle and instruct the class members to watch the candle melt away as they think about their fears also melting away.

If you do not want to wait for an entire candle to burn out, let it burn for a while and then open a window quickly. Watch the smoke either go straight up in the air or out the window. So much for fears.

AND GOD SAID, "IT IS GOOD."

3. Anger

Focusing Scripture

> *Let the words of my mouth and the meditation of my heart*
> *be acceptable to you,*
> *O LORD, my rock and my redeemer.*

(PSALM 19:14)

To Think About

Intense anger is a feeling that all of us have known. Even Jesus felt its power surging up in him: "[Jesus] looked around at them with anger; he was grieved at their hardness of heart" (Mark 3:5).

Rage is an overpowering emotion, and sometimes children do not know what to do with it. Share the following information with your class to suggest a place and a method for them to let out their rage.

Say: Sometimes we need to let go of anger. Nature is a good place to vent our intense feelings. Nature can take it. Beat on the rocks—they are strong. Stomp on the earth. It will not crumble. Cry and shout to the trees. They will not fall. Fight the ocean surf. It will keep coming. You cannot harm it. Fall down sobbing. Nature is there, ready to comfort our weeping. And when our anger is spent, birds sing and insects hum. The universe continues. We are enfolded in something far bigger than ourselves.

We become aware that God does not take us out of the world. The hurt and the pain are still there, but God helps us live through it, and our problems seem smaller, our fears more bearable. Warm and gentle thoughts can exorcise hate and anger. Look around in nature for the gentle things: a baby animal, the feel of moss, the smell of apple blossoms.

Nature is always here, reminding us that God is always with us. Spring comes, then summer blossoms. Autumn brings harvest; winter, sharp cold. We relax our human arrogance and go on. Nature reminds us again and again of our source, our true home and our small, swiftly passing place in it all. Every morning—the sun. Every night—the stars. Read Psalm 102:25-27:

> Long ago you laid the foundation of the earth
>> and the heavens are the work of your hands.
> They will perish, but you endure;
>> they will all wear out like a garment.
> You change them like clothing, and they pass away;
>> but you are the same, and your years have no end.

Activity

The first musical instruments came from nature. An animal skin stretched over a log was the first drum. An animal horn foreshadowed the brass instruments. A bone with a hole to blow through, a stalk of hollow grass, a whittled piece of wood—these were the first pipes.

Take the class to an outdoor area to discover something in nature with which to make music. Have each student "find" a percussion instrument.

Back in the classroom, use these natural "instruments" in an impromptu musical arrangement, to release any pain or anger that might be in their hearts.

Say: Beat as loudly as you can! The power of God protects you!

AND GOD SAID, "IT IS GOOD."

4. Busyness

Focusing Scripture

> *Remember the sabbath day, and keep it holy.*
> (EXODUS 20:8)

To Think About

Martin Luther once said, "This is an especially busy day. I have an unusual amount of things to do. I will pray an extra hour." The paradox expressed here is that the busier and more crowded our day, the greater our need to stop and spend time alone with God.

One of the most puzzling issues facing us in the church is the use of the sabbath. You will find children who do not even know what the word means, much less that its observance is one of the Ten Commandments of God. Is sabbath observance an outmoded ritual, or a sacred Commandment? We are becoming as busy on Sunday—both inside and outside the church—as on any other day of the week.

Activity

The following skit is suggested for raising this issue with your class. It may be done with three characters and a narrator doing the entire thing, or it may be done spontaneously, with the characters and narrator reading their parts and the rest of the group making the suggested movements.

A SABBATH FABLE

Characters
Narrator: tells the story
Zipp 1 and Zipp 2: few words and lots of pantomime action
B. S. (Beautiful Stranger): uses basket with props, or simply pantomimes

Narrator: Once upon a time, there was a land called Zippadaland. The people of this land were noted for their speed and efficiency and hard work. (*Zipps 1 and 2 enter*)
   People from other lands looked at Zippadaland in amazement and envy—at the products it produced (*Zipps move hands back and forth swiftly as if pulling a lever*) and the speed at which it produced them. (*Zipps move hands round and round swiftly as if turning a wheel*)
   The people of Zippadaland became proud of their reputation and began to work harder and harder (*lever motion*) and faster and faster. (*wheel motion*)
   And a strange thing began to happen to the people. If someone said:
Zipp 1: Good morning!
   the other would look at that person strangely and hurry on. (*Zipp 2 pantomimes motion*)
   There was no time to say, "Good morning." And after a while, they could no longer talk. And if someone said:
Zipp 2: Hear that bird sing!
   the other would look at that person strangely and hurry on. There was no time to listen. (*Zipp 1 pantomimes motion*)
   They lived in a prickly, machine-humming world, and after a while they could not hear. It took too long to say:
Zipp 1: I'm sorry.
   and people forgot how to feel, and their faces became frozen in a hostile stare. (*Zipps pantomime*)
   And it took too long to say:
Zipp 2: Thank you.
   So people just grabbed what they needed and hurried on. (*pantomime motions*)
   No one took time to ponder and think, and after a while they forgot how to sit, because their legs were always moving. (*pantomime*)
   And they became more and more like robots—making lots of products (*lever motion*) and making them very fast. (*wheel motion*)
   One day a beautiful stranger came to the land. (*Girl with basket skips in*)
   It grieved her to see what was happening to the people of Zippadaland. Now, this beautiful stranger had a basket of magic. (*hold up basket*)

And she decided to help the people. First she scattered magic dust from her basket *(scatter confetti, or pantomime)* and the people began to slow down. *(Zipps 1 and 2 pantomime)*

When they slowed down, she placed a magic potion on their eyes. *(giant clown sunglasses or make giant glasses with your fingers)*

And they began to look and see all the beauty around them. *(pantomime)*

They were so thrilled with what they saw that they sat down to look more closely. They were creaky and stiff, and at first it was hard to do. *(pantomime)*

When they were seated, the beautiful stranger took out a book. It was a Bible! She began to read to them. They listened with amazement, and their ears began to open again. *(hit side of heads, shake heads)*

And then one said in a creaky voice:

Zipp 1: Thank you.

The other looked in astonishment. Then he tried it, too:

Zipp 2: Thank you.

Next the beautiful stranger took something else from her basket—kazoos! And they began to play together, and smiles broke through their stiff faces, and they began to dance and laugh. *(use real kazoos or pantomime)*

They were having so much fun, they did not notice that the beautiful stranger had stood up. As the last thing from her basket, she took out a note. *(B.S. leaves note and tiptoes out)*

After a while they noticed she was gone. They picked up the note and read:

Zipp 1: Remember that you are human beings, not human doings.

    (Zipp 2 scratches head in puzzlement. Then both go back to playing their kazoos.)

The people of Zippadaland still work very hard and very fast for six days. But on one day every week, they stop and look and listen and say, "Thank you," and remember and play kazoos.

Leader: Think about this: As in everything in our lives, we need moderation. Work is basic and fundamental and good, but carried to the extreme, it becomes greed and obsession. We need a sabbath to revive, to rearrange our days, to ponder what is important in life, and to give thanks to God. "Those who wait for the LORD shall renew their strength" (Isa. 40:31).

AND GOD SAID, "IT IS GOOD."

5. An Evening Walk

Focusing Scripture

> *You make darkness, and it is night,*
>   *when all the animals of the forest come creeping out.*
>   (PSALM 104:20)

To Think About

A night walk is an interesting nature experience for your class. New wonders are there for your exploring. Take along a flashlight that has its lens covered with a piece of red cellophane. This light will not startle resident wildlife, and you may get closer and see more. Instruct the class to wear dark clothing in order to blend with the background and to walk softly.

Activity

Lead the way quietly. Night creatures are shy, but if you are very lucky you might see:

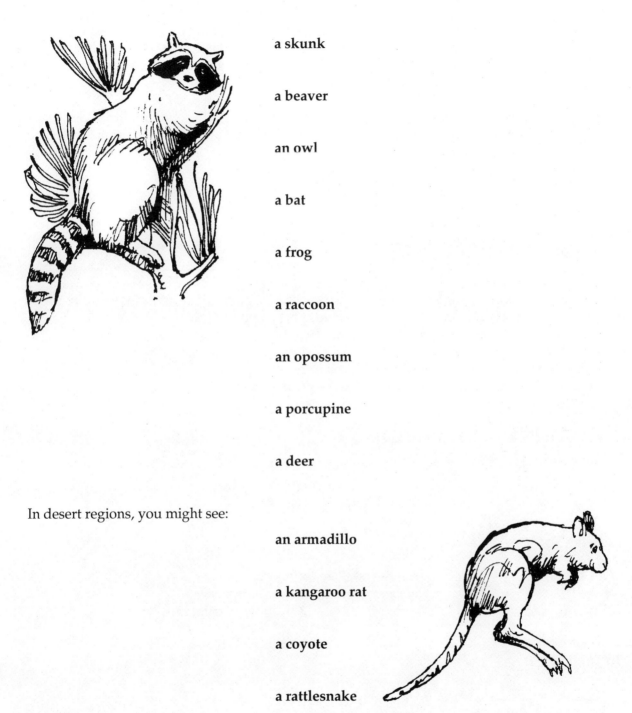

a skunk

a beaver

an owl

a bat

a frog

a raccoon

an opossum

a porcupine

a deer

In desert regions, you might see:

an armadillo

a kangaroo rat

a coyote

a rattlesnake

Are there different night creatures in your area? How many can you see? Perhaps you will see only the reflection of shining eyes in the darkness, or hear only the rustle of an animal scurrying away.

You also will want to notice the plant life at night. It is amazing to see how it has changed since you saw it in the daylight. Can you find:
- flowers that are shut up tight?
- flowers that open at night (e.g., moonflowers or evening primroses)?
- flowers with heavy night scents? Many are white and stand out in the darkness.

Be aware of sounds like rustling leaves, or bird or insect cries, but also listen to the night silence. There is an underneath-all sound—a silent pulsing that is difficult to hear. Listen, and become aware of the sort of silence in which you can hear the swish of falling stars or the sound of the earth's heartbeat.

Close your eyes occasionally and sniff. Smells are more pronounced at night. Walking through a woods, smell the air sharp with the scent of resin. Be aware of the wind and breezes. Feel them. Sniff the aromas they bring. Breathe deeply of the bracing evening air and the exhilaration it brings.

Can you find an open place that will give you a full panorama of the night sky? Standing there and looking up, say Psalm 8:3-4:

> When I look at your heavens, the work of your fingers,
>   the moon and the stars which you have established;
> what are human beings that you are mindful of them,
>   mortals that you care for them?

Open yourself to the wonder—the reverence and love we feel in the presence of the inscrutable universe. Consider the stars as witnesses of God's sovereignty and as signs of God's power.

Back in the classroom, reflect on the experience. After sharing discoveries, invite the students to sit quietly with their eyes closed. Say: Think of your life as a night walk.
- It makes us feel secure to have a good leader. Jesus is our leader.
- It is more fun to go with a group, sharing discoveries. The church is our group.
- A flashlight illuminates the way. The Bible is our flashlight.
- God is with us always, everywhere. This is the great good news. And God is not just with us, but going on ahead of us.

AND GOD SAID, "IT IS GOOD."

6. To View the Stars

Focusing Scripture

> *The heavens are telling the glory of God;*
> *and the firmament proclaims his handiwork.*
>
> (PSALM 19:1)

To Think About

Evening makes us aware of the boundlessness of the night sky. We are aware of how close, cluttered, and crowded our houses are, as we step outdoors and look up. We are dwarfed by the majestic beauty of the star-filled sky. Space seems lonely and vast beyond our conception. Under these countless stars, we sense our true size.

On a clear evening when the sky seems close, go outdoors with your class. Invite them to look quietly, absorbing the scene.

Say: At first, all the stars may look alike. But keep looking. Some will soon appear brighter. You might even be able to detect some colors . . . white . . . red . . . blue . . . yellow. Look for the Milky Way. It is made up of billions and billions of stars. This is hard for the mind to grasp. Can you find it?

Can you pick out one star that is slowly moving—hinting of eons of time and the vast spaces through which we hurtle? Think about this: The stars we see today are the same ones seen by people thousands and thousands of years ago.

Share space experiences. **Ask:** What wonders have you seen? A shooting star? A brilliant meteor? These last for only a few seconds. Maybe you have seen a comet, with its wispy cloudlike tail. Ancient people believed that a comet was the finger of God pointing toward earth, telling people to beware. Can you pick out the planets?

Spend some quiet time just looking into the sky. Wonders are there to be seen.

Activity

Create a quartos book. Back in the classroom, tell the students that since our logical minds cannot grasp the vastness of the universe, we will use our imaginations.

Give each student a large piece of typing paper. Instruct them to fold it in half, and then in half again, to make four pages. On the first page, write: "I went out to meet God in space, and _____." Continue on the second page. At the top of the third page, write: "And then _____." On the last page, write: "Finally, _____."

Tell the students to use their imaginations to fill in the blanks. They are to limit their writing to the size of the page. This will help them condense and bring together their thoughts. To start their writing, you might suggest:

- Imagine leaving the earth altogether. What would that be like?
- Imagine coming to the stars and beholding their orderly array. What would that be like?
- Imagine coming to the immovable power beyond the stars, which guides and controls all things. What would that be like?
- Imagine coming to a place that is unchangeable, a place that is eternal, that exists in its own right.
- Imagine going outside of time, even beyond time itself—beyond anything that ever was. Who would you meet, and what would you say?

Instruct the students to put something of themselves on the paper—their ideas, their imaginations, their personalities. Share these stories.

AND GOD SAID, "IT IS GOOD."

7. A Bedtime Story

Focusing Scripture

> *To you is born this day in the city of David a Savior, who is the Messiah, the Lord.*
>
> (LUKE 2:11)

To Think About

Probably the most beloved evening story in our Bible is the story of Jesus' birth. Read it again to become aware of all the nature images. You will find the stories in Luke 2:1-10 and in Matthew 2:1-12.

Though the actual date is uncertain, we think of Christmas as happening in midwinter when the days are darkest. At that time, came the Light of the world.

The Christmas story is an interesting juxtaposition of the cosmic and the earthly. Earthly shepherds heard heavenly angels. In an earthly stable, the Incarnation occurred. And the message that comes through is that all of life is holy, that even our everyday existence can be shot through with miracles. Our taken-for-granted daily realities may in fact be filled with heavenly surprises.

Though a manger, sheep, and stars are the only nature images actually mentioned in the Bible, many legends have arisen that link and interlink nature objects with the Christmas story.

These legends are not just charming stories, but on the level that they pick up some characteristic or theme from Jesus' life, they are true. We look to nature images to help us understand Christmas messages in a new way, to help us find God where we are. Tell this story to your class:

Have you heard the legend of the robin? Long ago on that first Christmas night, a small brown bird was perched on a beam in a stable in Bethlehem, watching people come to worship the newborn Christ Child. It was a very simple, plain bird, and no one took much notice of it.

After all the visitors had left and the Holy Family settled down to sleep, the little bird saw that the fire built to keep the baby Jesus warm was dying out. So the bird flew down and fanned the coals with its wings, fanning with all its might, till its little heart beat hard and fast.

Soon the fire became brighter and warmer, and the feathers on the bird's breast began to glow a brilliant red. Though very weary, the bird stayed by the fire all night, fanning it to keep the blaze bright and the Christ Child warm.

Legend tells us that since that first Christmas night, the robin has had a red breast, a symbol of its love for the baby in the manger.

Ask the class: What is the Christmas message here? How was the little bird like Jesus?

The little robin, like Jesus, was self-giving and recognized the demands of love. How could you be like the robin?

An icon is an object we look at or think about in order to better understand God. The robin, through this story, becomes an icon for us. Remembering the story, we recall again the characteristics of Jesus and, by extension, the way of life he patterned for us—a way of acting and living in the world, a graced way of responding to life.

Activity

1. Make a banner that says: "Truth is sometimes known before it is fully understood," and cover the banner with robins.

2. Around Christmastime, there are often small artificial birds for sale. Perch robins all over a sturdy tree branch as a reminder of this legend, a Christmas message from nature.

AND GOD SAID, "IT IS GOOD."

8. Angels' Wings

Focusing Scripture

> *For he will command his angels concerning you*
> *to guard you in all your ways.*
>
> (PSALM 91:11)

To Think About

This is one of several nature activities that can take place even in the innner city. On a rooftop above a city, children can become aware of soft wind, clouds, stars. The soft wings of birds can be heard.

Activity

With the children seated in a circle, pass around some soft objects: a pillow, a teddy bear, a baby blanket.

Ask the class to feel the pillow. As you pass the teddy bear, ask: "Did you ever have a teddy bear?" Invite the children to feel it, hug it. Ask: "What did you take to bed with you as a little child? Did you have a special blanket?" Pass around the blanket. Ask the children to touch all these objects gently and reverently.

Now pass around some hard objects—for example, a football helmet and a brick. Invite the children to feel these objects.

Tell the children that sometimes God's protection of us is strong, but tonight we are thinking about God's soft protection. God's protection surrounds us with goodness, gentleness, kindness, and acceptance. Encourage the children to find that softness in themselves.

Say the Bible verse above, and ask the children if they can picture large wings of angels keeping them safe. Now invite them to close their eyes. Say:

Make believe large wings of angels are holding you.

Make believe you are taking something you fear and tucking it in an angel's wing.
Make believe you are placing your hand in the soft fold of an angel's wing.
Imagine that angels are soft mysteries, surrounding you.

With these images in our mind, we learn this Bible verse: "I will both lie down and sleep in peace; for you alone, O LORD, make me lie down in safety" (Ps. 4:8).

A last thought: God continually broods over us and warms us. We can relax in the assurance that we are cherished. Hug yourself and smile.

AND GOD SAID, "IT IS GOOD."

9. Death

Focusing Scripture

> *Where, O death, is your victory?*
> *Where, O death, is your sting?*
>
> (I CORINTHIANS 15:55)

To Think About

And now we come to the final letting go—death. Most of us tend to agree with poet Edna St. Vincent Millay, who said about death, "Despite the evidence, I am not resigned."

We refuse to accept the fact that all of us will die. Again, nature can be a great teacher and comfort to us here.

Rather than having one specific nature activity that deals with death, or one occasion when we solemnly and seriously discuss death with the class, it would be better to be sensitive to this area of a child's spiritual growth and use short moments and experiences to plant seeds of trust and hope. Accept their fears, but tell them again and again that we can trust beyond our fears.

Teaching opportunities will arise. Read the following information about nature and death, and decide where you agree or disagree. When our own feelings are clear, they will surface in our teaching.

Life is a process, a movement of continually reshaping forms. We can hold nothing still. Nature proclaims this message over and over again—the seed, the blossom, the pod, the dying, the new seed, the new blossom—and so on and on. All parts of nature teach that the passing away of one life is the making of room for another. Not only in dying but in all of life, we push on to the next movement, no longer clutching to the past, holding on to a life that is over.

Naturalist John Muir believed that God's love was the central message of all nature and that death itself is merely a transition point, when beauty changes its form. He gave the examples of snowflakes melting to form a mirror lake, a doe dying to nourish a wild orchid. This orderly progression of nature from one form of beauty to another, he believed, demonstrates God's love for the whole world. Alienation from nature, Muir thought, is what causes our fear of death and our blindness to the Creator's message of love.

Activity

Looking with a child through a kaleidoscope is a fun experience. We can, in a simple way, connect this experience with death by commenting on the beauty of the continually reshaping forms. We can hold nothing still. Life is a process.

Watching a sunrise with a child, we can affirm that a day with morning, noon, and sunset is a beautiful arrangement—like our lives with birth, activity, and death.

Walking with your class through an old cemetery—peaceful, quiet, and lovely—can be a good way to begin talking together about death. Invite the students to remember when they first heard about death, where they were, and how they felt about it. Accept the feelings as normal and natural.

When you are walking with your class out in the natural world, observe the beautiful blendings of death and life. A fallen tree is a good example. You can observe the tree that once sprouted leaves and now is decaying to dust, which in turn will nourish the earth and produce new trees. Feel, with your class, these various stages. Feel the hardness of the remaining trunk. Sift the dust through your fingers. Smell it. Is it wet or dry? Look for tiny green sprouts of new life. Touch them, and experience a joyous inseparable unity. The Creator intended it to be this way. It reminds us that one day we too will die.

When we accept that all life on earth is precarious, transient, and fleeting, we become aware of its richness, color and joy.

And the resurrection of Jesus breaks through this beautiful plan of God's with even more promise. If love is at the heart of creation, God's supreme act of love in Christ's death is its demonstration. Jesus opened for us the curtain, showing us that continuity and personhood are also part of God's ongoing plan for us. It is a great mystery. We believe that Jesus is the Christ, God's chosen One for the world, and through him we receive eternal life.

There is nothing left to fear when we truly let ourselves go, yielding to the larger plan of God.

AND GOD SAID, "IT IS GOOD."

EVENING

Letting Go

Do not worry about tomorrow,
for tomorrow will bring worries of its own.
(MATTHEW 6:34)

When I am afraid
I put my trust in you.
(PSALM 56:3)

Remember the sabbath day,
and keep it holy.
(EXODUS 20:8)

You make darkness, and it is night,
when all the animals of the forest
come creeping out.
(PSALM 104:20)

The heavens are telling the glory of God;
and the firmament proclaims his handiwork.
(PSALM 19:1)

He will command his angels concerning you
to guard you in all your ways.
(PSALM 91:11)

SCRIPTURE INDEX